CONTE

CONTENTS

JUMBLE

Unscramble the Jumbles, one letter to each space, to form Bible words.

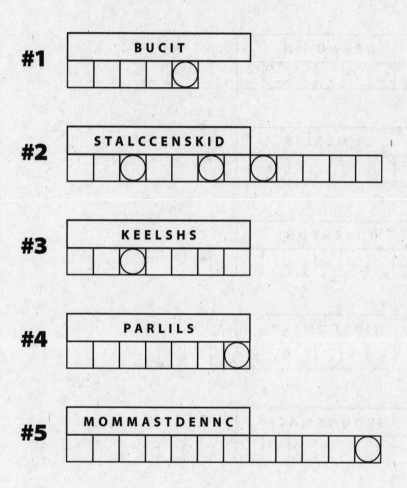

#1 BUCIT

#2 STALCCENSKID

#3 KEELSHS

#4 PARLILS

#5 MOMMASTDENNC

Now, arrange the circled letters to solve the Mystery Answer, suggested by the Jumble words.

MYSTERY ANSWER:

O F

JUMBLE

Unscramble the Jumbles, one letter to each space, to form Bible words.

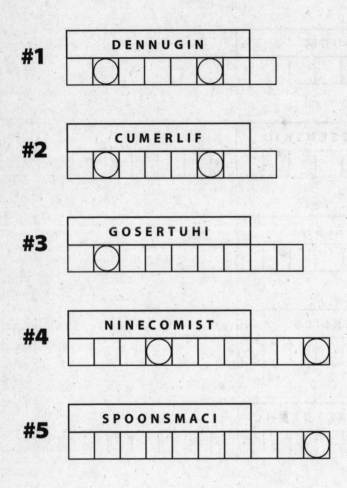

#1 DENNUGIN

#2 CUMERLIF

#3 GOSERTUHI

#4 NINECOMIST

#5 SPOONSMACI

Now, arrange the circled letters to solve the Mystery Answer, suggested by the Jumble words.

MYSTERY ANSWER:

JUMBLE

Unscramble the Jumbles, one letter to each space, to form Bible words.

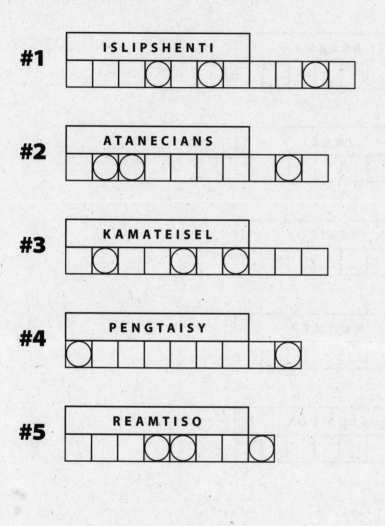

#1 ISLIPSHENTI

#2 ATANECIANS

#3 KAMATEISEL

#4 PENGTAISY

#5 REAMTISO

Now, arrange the circled letters to solve the Mystery Answer, suggested by the Jumble words.

MYSTERY ANSWER:

JUMBLE

Unscramble the Jumbles, one letter to each space, to form Bible words.

#1 ATARRA

#2 INASI

#3 VELISO

#4 NOHMER

#5 SLUMPOY

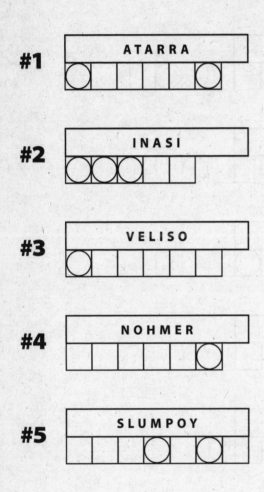

Now, arrange the circled letters to solve the Mystery Answer, suggested by the Jumble words.

MYSTERY ANSWER:

JUMBLE

Unscramble the Jumbles, one letter to each space, to form Bible words.

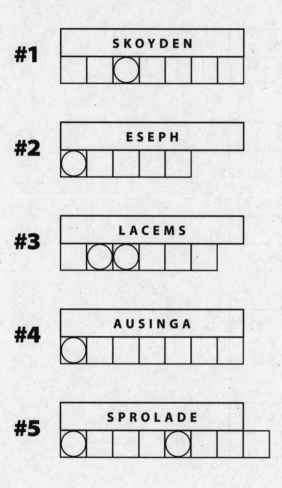

#1 SKOYDEN

#2 ESEPH

#3 LACEMS

#4 AUSINGA

#5 SPROLADE

Now, arrange the circled letters to solve the Mystery Answer, suggested by the Jumble words.

MYSTERY ANSWER:

JUMBLE

Unscramble the Jumbles, one letter to each space, to form Bible words.

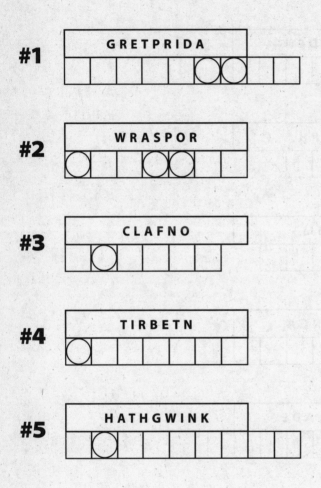

#1 GRETPRIDA

#2 WRASPOR

#3 CLAFNO

#4 TIRBETN

#5 HATHGWINK

Now, arrange the circled letters to solve the Mystery Answer, suggested by the Jumble words.

MYSTERY ANSWER:

O F   T H E

JUMBLE

Unscramble the Jumbles, one letter to each space, to form Bible words.

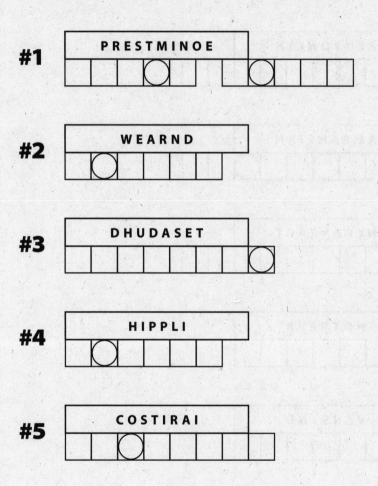

#1 PRESTMINOE

#2 WEARND

#3 DHUDASET

#4 HIPPLI

#5 COSTIRAI

Now, arrange the circled letters to solve the Mystery Answer, suggested by the Jumble words.

MYSTERY ANSWER:

JUMBLE

Unscramble the Jumbles, one letter to each space, to form Bible words.

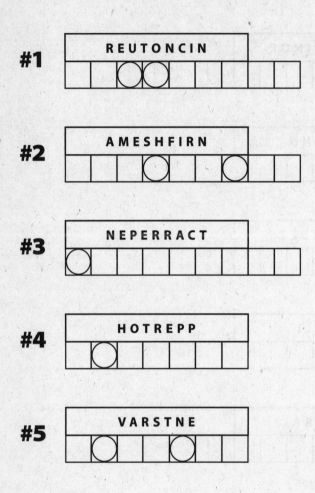

#1 REUTONCIN

#2 AMESHFIRN

#3 NEPERRACT

#4 HOTREPP

#5 VARSTNE

Now, arrange the circled letters to solve the Mystery Answer, suggested by the Jumble words.

MYSTERY ANSWER:

JUMBLE

Unscramble the Jumbles, one letter to each space, to form Bible words.

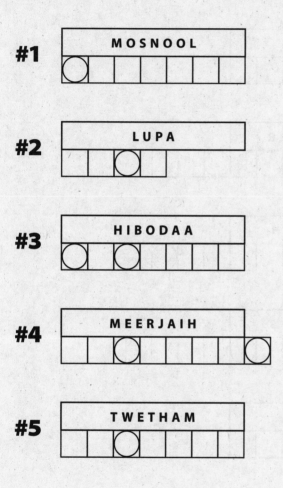

#1 MOSNOOL

#2 LUPA

#3 HIBODAA

#4 MEERJAIH

#5 TWETHAM

Now, arrange the circled letters to solve the Mystery Answer, suggested by the Jumble words.

MYSTERY ANSWER:

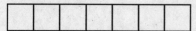

JUMBLE

Unscramble the Jumbles, one letter to each space, to form Bible words.

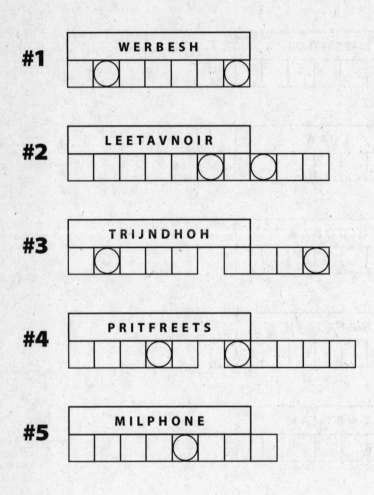

#1 WERBESH

#2 LEETAVNOIR

#3 TRIJNDHOH

#4 PRITFREETS

#5 MILPHONE

Now, arrange the circled letters to solve the Mystery Answer, suggested by the Jumble words.

MYSTERY ANSWER:

JUMBLE

Unscramble the Jumbles, one letter to each space, to form Bible words.

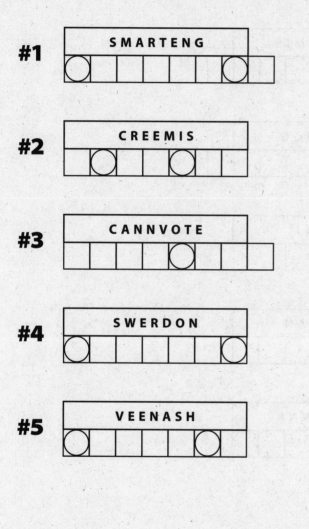

#1 SMARTENG

#2 CREEMIS

#3 CANNVOTE

#4 SWERDON

#5 VEENASH

Now, arrange the circled letters to solve the Mystery Answer, suggested by the Jumble words.

MYSTERY ANSWER:

JUMBLE

Unscramble the Jumbles, one letter to each space, to form Bible words.

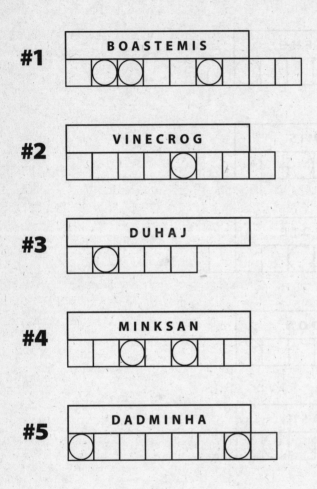

#1 BOASTEMIS

#2 VINECROG

#3 DUHAJ

#4 MINKSAN

#5 DADMINHA

Now, arrange the circled letters to solve the Mystery Answer, suggested by the Jumble words.

MYSTERY ANSWER:

A N D

JUMBLE

Unscramble the Jumbles, one letter to each space, to form Bible words.

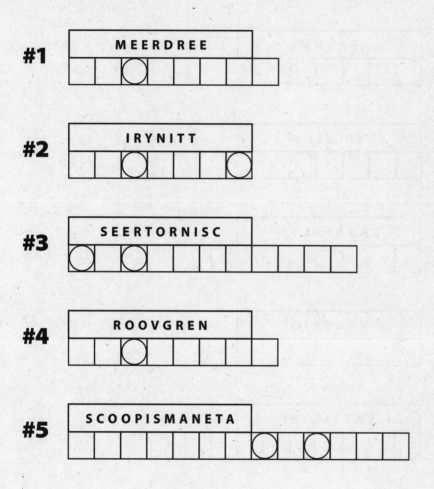

#1 MEERDREE

#2 IRYNITT

#3 SEERTORNISC

#4 ROOVGREN

#5 SCOOPISMANETA

Now, arrange the circled letters to solve the Mystery Answer, suggested by the Jumble words.

MYSTERY ANSWER:

JUMBLE

Unscramble the Jumbles, one letter to each space, to form Bible words.

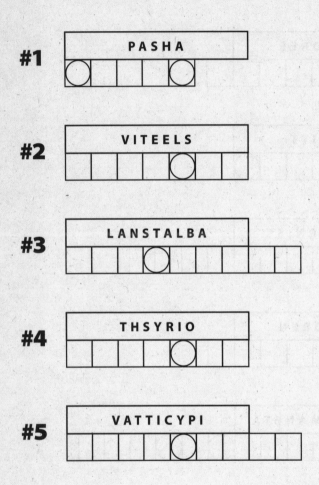

#1 PASHA

#2 VITEELS

#3 LANSTALBA

#4 THSYRIO

#5 VATTICYPI

Now, arrange the circled letters to solve the Mystery Answer, suggested by the Jumble words.

MYSTERY ANSWER:

JUMBLE

Unscramble the Jumbles, one letter to each space, to form Bible words.

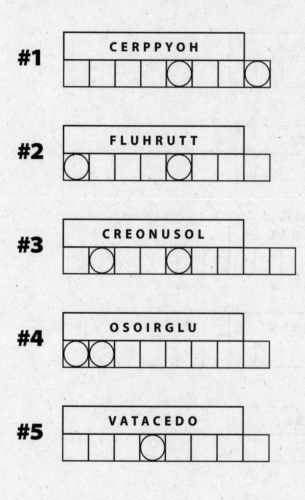

#1 CERPPYOH

#2 FLUHRUTT

#3 CREONUSOL

#4 OSOIRGLU

#5 VATACEDO

Now, arrange the circled letters to solve the Mystery Answer, suggested by the Jumble words.

MYSTERY ANSWER:

JUMBLE

Unscramble the Jumbles, one letter to each space, to form Bible words.

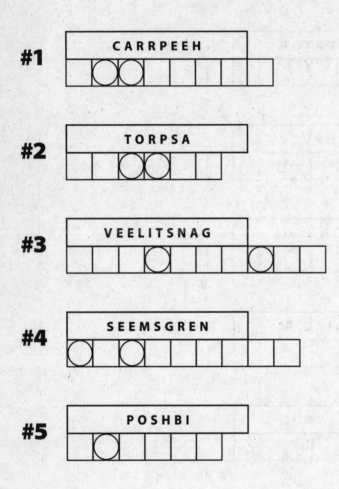

#1 CARRPEEH

#2 TORPSA

#3 VEELITSNAG

#4 SEEMSGREN

#5 POSHBI

Now, arrange the circled letters to solve the Mystery Answer, suggested by the Jumble words.

MYSTERY ANSWER:

JUMBLE

Unscramble the Jumbles, one letter to each space, to form Bible words.

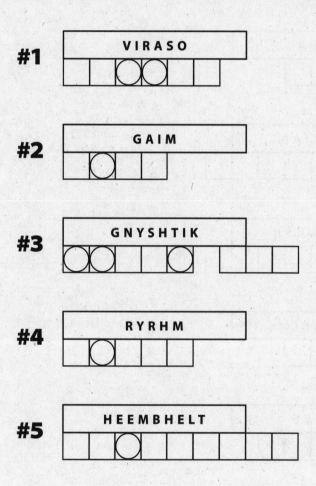

#1 VIRASO

#2 GAIM

#3 GNYSHTIK

#4 RYRHM

#5 HEEMBHELT

Now, arrange the circled letters to solve the Mystery Answer, suggested by the Jumble words.

MYSTERY ANSWER:

JUMBLE

Unscramble the Jumbles, one letter to each space, to form Bible words.

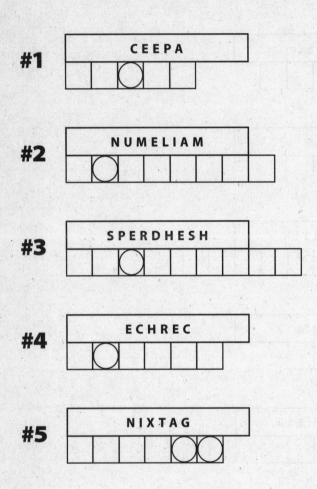

#1 CEEPA

#2 NUMELIAM

#3 SPERDHESH

#4 ECHREC

#5 NIXTAG

Now, arrange the circled letters to solve the Mystery Answer, suggested by the Jumble words.

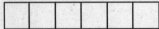

MYSTERY ANSWER:

JUMBLE

Unscramble the Jumbles, one letter to each space, to form Bible words.

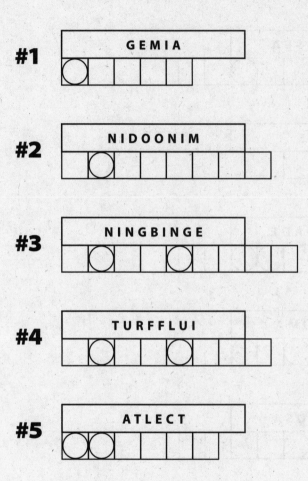

#1 GEMIA

#2 NIDOONIM

#3 NINGBINGE

#4 TURFFLUI

#5 ATLECT

Now, arrange the circled letters to solve the Mystery Answer, suggested by the Jumble words.

MYSTERY ANSWER:

JUMBLE

Unscramble the Jumbles, one letter to each space, to form Bible words.

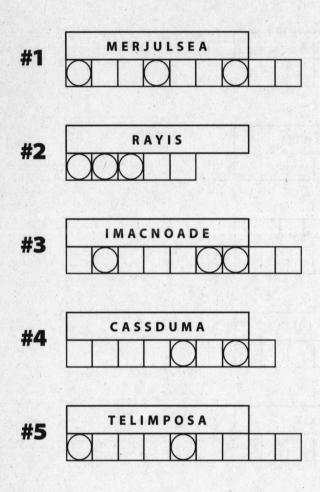

#1 MERJULSEA

#2 RAYIS

#3 IMACNOADE

#4 CASSDUMA

#5 TELIMPOSA

Now, arrange the circled letters to solve the Mystery Answer, suggested by the Jumble words.

MYSTERY ANSWER:

JUMBLE

Unscramble the Jumbles, one letter to each space, to form Bible words.

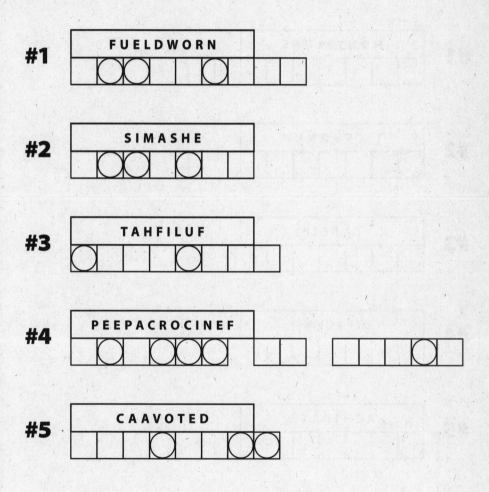

#1 FUELDWORN

#2 SIMASHE

#3 TAHFILUF

#4 PEEPACROCINEF

#5 CAAVOTED

Now, arrange the circled letters to solve the Mystery Answer, suggested by the Jumble words.

MYSTERY ANSWER:

JUMBLE

Unscramble the Jumbles, one letter to each space, to form Bible words.

#1 HOHTIXURS

#2 TICERONUN

#3 TAELIP

#4 IFILVY

#5 ACHIPASA

Now, arrange the circled letters to solve the Mystery Answer, suggested by the Jumble words.

MYSTERY ANSWER:

JUMBLE

Unscramble the Jumbles, one letter to each space, to form Bible words.

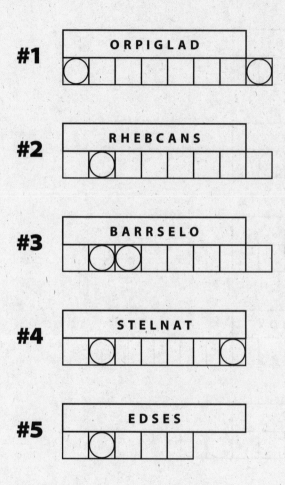

#1 ORPIGLAD

#2 RHEBCANS

#3 BARRSELO

#4 STELNAT

#5 EDSES

Now, arrange the circled letters to solve the Mystery Answer, suggested by the Jumble words.

MYSTERY ANSWER:

JUMBLE

Unscramble the Jumbles, one letter to each space, to form Bible words.

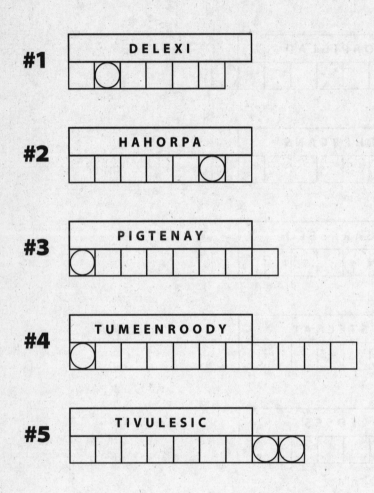

#1 DELEXI

#2 HAHORPA

#3 PIGTENAY

#4 TUMEENROODY

#5 TIVULESIC

Now, arrange the circled letters to solve the Mystery Answer, suggested by the Jumble words.

MYSTERY ANSWER:

JUMBLE

Unscramble the Jumbles, one letter to each space, to form Bible words.

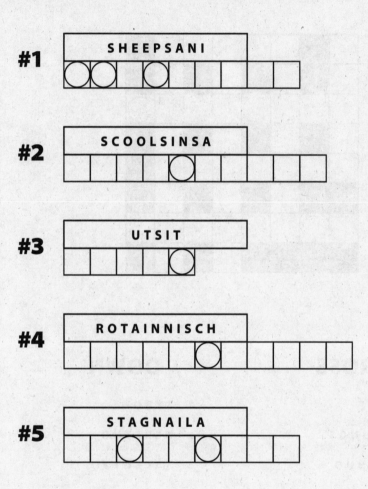

#1 SHEEPSANI

#2 SCOOLSINSA

#3 UTSIT

#4 ROTAINNISCH

#5 STAGNAILA

Now, arrange the circled letters to solve the Mystery Answer, suggested by the Jumble words.

MYSTERY ANSWER:

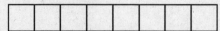

CRISS-CROSS JUMBLE

Complete the crossword puzzle by unscrambling the Jumbles to form ordinary words.

ACROSS

2 CUSOF

5 TRIBUNGS

6 REYGNUO

7 REERHICS

DOWN

1 BYBOH

2 NERFTUO

3 RACEGTYO

4 TREESNSI

When the puzzle is complete, unscramble the circled letters to find the Mystery Answer.

MYSTERY ANSWER:

CRISS-CROSS JUMBLE

Complete the crossword puzzle by unscrambling the Jumbles to form ordinary words.

ACROSS

2 EYNIDITT

6 CESTEFF

7 LYRAL

8 SISER

DOWN

1 CORTRIDE

3 REFOFST

4 KLASTEC

5 YASTT

When the puzzle is complete, unscramble the circled letters to find the Mystery Answer.

MYSTERY ANSWER:

27

CRISS-CROSS JUMBLE

Complete the crossword puzzle by unscrambling the Jumbles to form ordinary words.

ACROSS

1 PEKREES

5 NUGOTHE

6 IGSWT

7 GRESTULG

DOWN

1 NEKTSTI

2 TAUQORE

3 NEHOGIC

4 NUISS

When the puzzle is complete, unscramble the circled letters to find the Mystery Answer.

MYSTERY ANSWER:

CRISS-CROSS JUMBLE

Complete the crossword puzzle by unscrambling the Jumbles to form ordinary words.

ACROSS

1 LIBDUGIN

4 GINANERL

6 REVITALN

7 TEMESNIG

DOWN

1 MILGUBE

2 GELRATS

3 GELSOGG

5 TINNEV

When the puzzle is complete, unscramble the circled letters to find the Mystery Answer.

MYSTERY ANSWER:

CRISS-CROSS JUMBLE

Complete the crossword puzzle by unscrambling the Jumbles to form ordinary words.

ACROSS

1 BLOMSY

5 TFNEO

6 MOSOPHA

7 NUESSEPS

DOWN

1 CLOSSHAR

2 LUMPLITE

3 NOONSIIP

4 SEMSIS

When the puzzle is complete, unscramble the circled letters to find the Mystery Answer.

MYSTERY ANSWER:

CRISS-CROSS JUMBLE

Complete the crossword puzzle by unscrambling the Jumbles to form ordinary words.

ACROSS

1 PATSCE

4 FROMICN

5 DORFAF

6 SLEPHSEL

DOWN

1 ALUNALYN

2 LANIPUF

3 RECMAAS

4 GOCUSH

When the puzzle is complete, unscramble the circled letters to find the Mystery Answer.

MYSTERY ANSWER:

CRISS-CROSS JUMBLE

Complete the crossword puzzle by unscrambling the Jumbles to form ordinary words.

ACROSS

1 GRYROWNI

5 CINIDETA

6 DENEGNI

7 GIGWINNS

DOWN

1 WINTGISR

2 CUDEER

3 GHINATCY

4 GINNROTE

When the puzzle is complete, unscramble the circled letters to find the Mystery Answer.

MYSTERY ANSWER:

CRISS-CROSS JUMBLE

Complete the crossword puzzle by unscrambling the Jumbles to form ordinary words.

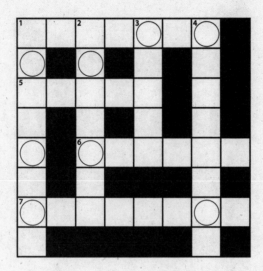

ACROSS

1 VALIVER

5 UFESS

6 LOBTET

7 DEETEUCX

DOWN

1 FRERDERE

2 LEVBISI

3 STIVI

4 INORELLE

When the puzzle is complete, unscramble the circled letters to find the Mystery Answer.

MYSTERY ANSWER:

CRISS-CROSS JUMBLE

Complete the crossword puzzle by unscrambling the Jumbles to form ordinary words.

ACROSS

1 NUETLOI

4 YURSONJE

6 PYACCAIT

7 RAASUDYT

DOWN

1 CJESBOT

2 PREMUTT

3 ENPAYTIG

5 CRINE

When the puzzle is complete, unscramble the circled letters to find the Mystery Answer.

MYSTERY ANSWER:

CRISS-CROSS JUMBLE

Complete the crossword puzzle by unscrambling the Jumbles to form ordinary words.

ACROSS

1 SORACEMP

5 COOMUTE

6 PLEYRROP

7 DOICS

DOWN

1 PHODPEC

2 HOMEDST

3 SOARE

4 YENLEV

When the puzzle is complete, unscramble the circled letters to find the Mystery Answer.

MYSTERY ANSWER:

CRISS-CROSS JUMBLE

Complete the crossword puzzle by unscrambling the Jumbles to form ordinary words.

ACROSS

2 MORST

4 SINEDI

6 SLIMFEH

7 KAPANSEC

DOWN

1 TUCKEPH

2 TEMPHINS

3 FIMEDDIO

5 SWEESA

When the puzzle is complete, unscramble the circled letters to find the Mystery Answer.

MYSTERY ANSWER:

CRISS-CROSS JUMBLE

Complete the crossword puzzle by unscrambling the Jumbles to form ordinary words.

ACROSS

1 HAINMUDO

6 TAGGEDS

7 GUTNINY

8 CUNOE

DOWN

2 LUNGDUE

3 DIDIOTAN

4 DEEBONIT

5 SEEGARID

When the puzzle is complete, unscramble the circled letters to find the Mystery Answer.

MYSTERY ANSWER:

CRISS-CROSS JUMBLE

Complete the crossword puzzle by unscrambling the Jumbles to form ordinary words.

ACROSS

2 KOMISSE

6 CESCAUS

7 TEEDSIP

8 DIDRENA

DOWN

1 WERRDDAE

3 SCIKK

4 ISIMNOS

5 SUDSNEP

When the puzzle is complete, unscramble the circled letters to find the Mystery Answer.

MYSTERY ANSWER:

CRISS-CROSS JUMBLE

Complete the crossword puzzle by unscrambling the Jumbles to form ordinary words.

ACROSS

1 DRATSOE

5 RUPALL

6 FARILLAN

7 NUSLEC

DOWN

1 REERTPOR

2 NUUMMILA

3 CRIFAFT

4 LESSHL

When the puzzle is complete, unscramble the circled letters to find the Mystery Answer.

MYSTERY ANSWER:

CRISS-CROSS JUMBLE

Complete the crossword puzzle by unscrambling the Jumbles to form ordinary words.

ACROSS

1 ELACERD

5 LUGPEA

6 ZEELAIR

7 NYANN

DOWN

1 GRINVOCE

2 PINEXAL

3 DYRALIE

4 EDUSO

When the puzzle is complete, unscramble the circled letters to find the Mystery Answer.

MYSTERY ANSWER:

CRISS-CROSS JUMBLE

Complete the crossword puzzle by unscrambling the Jumbles to form ordinary words.

ACROSS

1 GUNBLIBB

5 LASSNID

6 TRONAHE

7 SENNI

DOWN

1 TRIBINA

2 NOLOLBA

3 HULENSC

4 TRONSSLI

When the puzzle is complete, unscramble the circled letters to find the Mystery Answer.

MYSTERY ANSWER:

CRISS-CROSS JUMBLE

Complete the crossword puzzle by unscrambling the Jumbles to form ordinary words.

ACROSS

1 NEESHIC

5 DADDE

6 STENPICS

7 MREGS

DOWN

1 TAGOCNI

2 TYNIDSRU

3 NESDELS

4 UTOQANIE

When the puzzle is complete, unscramble the circled letters to find the Mystery Answer.

MYSTERY ANSWER:

CRISS-CROSS JUMBLE

Complete the crossword puzzle by unscrambling the Jumbles to form ordinary words.

ACROSS

1 PESACES

5 STITHR

6 VEENAGIT

7 PROSSPUT

DOWN

1 STEXDEN

2 GLINC

3 TOOSIPIN

4 DESEPS

When the puzzle is complete, unscramble the circled letters to find the Mystery Answer.

MYSTERY ANSWER:

CRISS-CROSS JUMBLE

Complete the crossword puzzle by unscrambling the Jumbles to form ordinary words.

ACROSS

2 ROSVEC

5 TIXCEO

6 WORRFDA

7 ZESSEQUE

DOWN

1 SHILDFOG

2 RHEULCEF

3 TEVILOA

4 REENRIDE

When the puzzle is complete, unscramble the circled letters to find the Mystery Answer.

MYSTERY ANSWER:

CRISS-CROSS JUMBLE

Complete the crossword puzzle by unscrambling the Jumbles to form ordinary words.

ACROSS

1 SACCLIS

5 NESLUTIO

6 DEEPLOV

7 GUNYO

DOWN

1 DRODWEC

2 VYAITICT

3 LLISST

4 PRECENGI

When the puzzle is complete, unscramble the circled letters to find the Mystery Answer.

MYSTERY ANSWER:

CRISS-CROSS JUMBLE

Complete the crossword puzzle by unscrambling the Jumbles to form ordinary words.

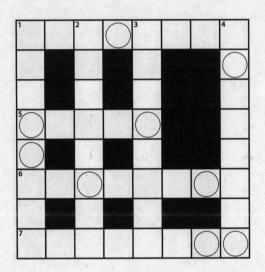

ACROSS

1 THAEPSEC

5 INMAS

6 DEXAPEND

7 DULNSDYE

DOWN

1 RIMLCEBS

2 PIQUEDEP

3 SEPERNEC

4 TRUASHDY

When the puzzle is complete, unscramble the circled letters to find the Mystery Answer.

MYSTERY ANSWER:

CRISS-CROSS JUMBLE

Complete the crossword puzzle by unscrambling the Jumbles to form ordinary words.

ACROSS

1 LITISCA

5 YELCIFER

6 DEDURSH

7 IXENCTT

DOWN

1 DEEFNITS

2 ATEEDAUQ

3 CINNTIDE

4 SLORA

When the puzzle is complete, unscramble the circled letters to find the Mystery Answer.

MYSTERY ANSWER:

CRISS-CROSS JUMBLE

Complete the crossword puzzle by unscrambling the Jumbles to form ordinary words.

ACROSS

2 SREDS

5 BLUSMEDT

7 RADLEEX

8 GUNXECSI

DOWN

1 REESBROV

3 DISPENNG

4 BILCUP

6 BEXSO

When the puzzle is complete, unscramble the circled letters to find the Mystery Answer.

MYSTERY ANSWER:

CRISS-CROSS JUMBLE

Complete the crossword puzzle by unscrambling the Jumbles to form ordinary words.

ACROSS

1 TYCAH

6 BLURMEAL

7 TEAMUSCH

8 STIRTUSO

DOWN

2 STOCCELL

3 REETSHAT

4 MISTUM

5 TWIERR

When the puzzle is complete, unscramble the circled letters to find the Mystery Answer.

MYSTERY ANSWER:

CRISS-CROSS JUMBLE

Complete the crossword puzzle by unscrambling the Jumbles to form ordinary words.

ACROSS

2 SLESRE

5 TULFFIAH

7 LENGUJ

8 SNEEKAWS

DOWN

1 SCILFF

3 FUEREGE

4 LUVAE

6 KRUTN

When the puzzle is complete, unscramble the circled letters to find the Mystery Answer.

MYSTERY ANSWER:

MYSTERY PERSON JUMBLE

Unscramble the Jumbles, one letter to each square, to form words that relate to the mystery person.

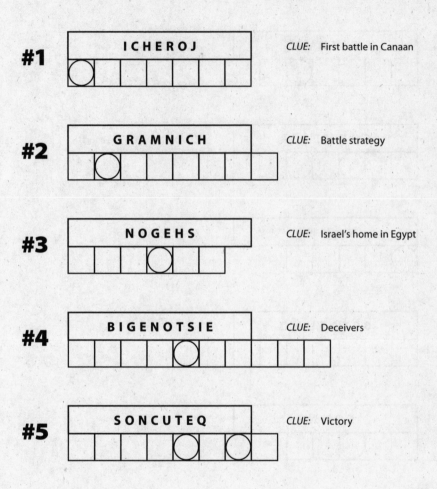

#1 ICHEROJ

CLUE: First battle in Canaan

#2 GRAMNICH

CLUE: Battle strategy

#3 NOGEHS

CLUE: Israel's home in Egypt

#4 BIGENOTSIE

CLUE: Deceivers

#5 SONCUTEQ

CLUE: Victory

Arrange the circled letters to solve the mystery person.

MYSTERY ANSWER:

MYSTERY PERSON JUMBLE

Unscramble the Jumbles, one letter to each square, to form words that relate to the mystery person.

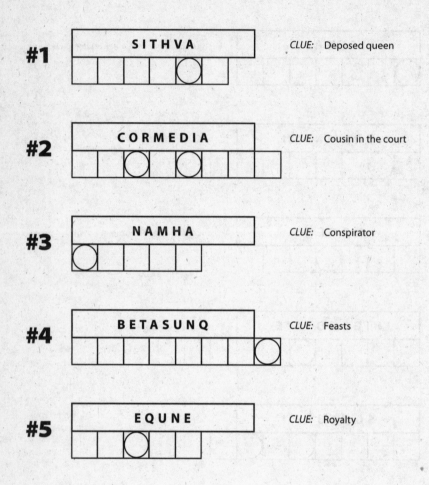

#1   S I T H V A   CLUE: Deposed queen

#2   C O R M E D I A   CLUE: Cousin in the court

#3   N A M H A   CLUE: Conspirator

#4   B E T A S U N Q   CLUE: Feasts

#5   E Q U N E   CLUE: Royalty

Arrange the circled letters to solve the mystery person.

MYSTERY ANSWER:

MYSTERY PERSON JUMBLE

Unscramble the Jumbles, one letter to each square, to form words that relate to the mystery person.

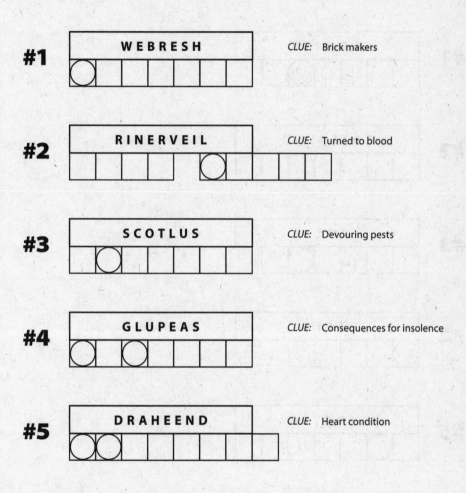

#1 WEBRESH

CLUE: Brick makers

#2 RINERVEIL

CLUE: Turned to blood

#3 SCOTLUS

CLUE: Devouring pests

#4 GLUPEAS

CLUE: Consequences for insolence

#5 DRAHEEND

CLUE: Heart condition

Arrange the circled letters to solve the mystery person.

MYSTERY ANSWER:

MYSTERY PERSON JUMBLE

Unscramble the Jumbles, one letter to each square, to form words that relate to the mystery person.

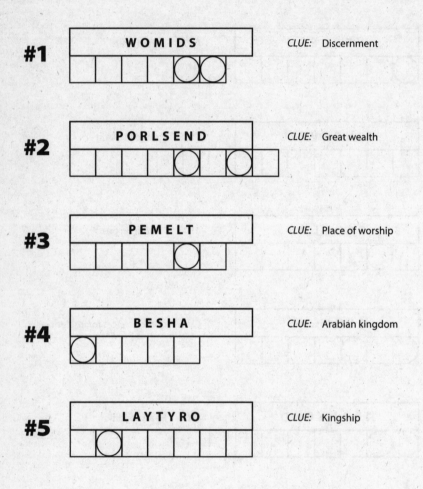

#1 W O M I D S CLUE: Discernment

#2 P O R L S E N D CLUE: Great wealth

#3 P E M E L T CLUE: Place of worship

#4 B E S H A CLUE: Arabian kingdom

#5 L A Y T Y R O CLUE: Kingship

Arrange the circled letters to solve the mystery person.

MYSTERY ANSWER:

MYSTERY PERSON JUMBLE

Unscramble the Jumbles, one letter to each square, to form words that relate to the mystery person.

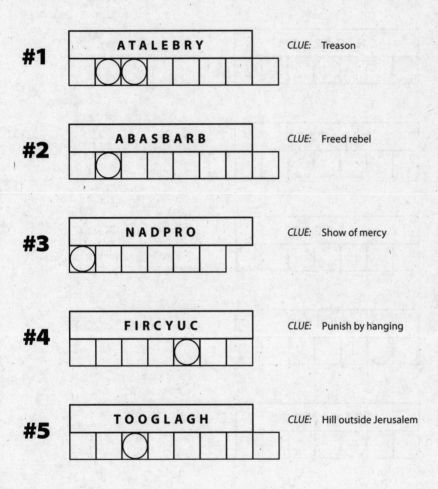

#1 ATALEBRY   CLUE: Treason

#2 ABASBARB   CLUE: Freed rebel

#3 NADPRO   CLUE: Show of mercy

#4 FIRCYUC   CLUE: Punish by hanging

#5 TOOGLAGH   CLUE: Hill outside Jerusalem

Arrange the circled letters to solve the mystery person.

MYSTERY ANSWER:

MYSTERY PERSON JUMBLE

Unscramble the Jumbles, one letter to each square, to form words that relate to the mystery person.

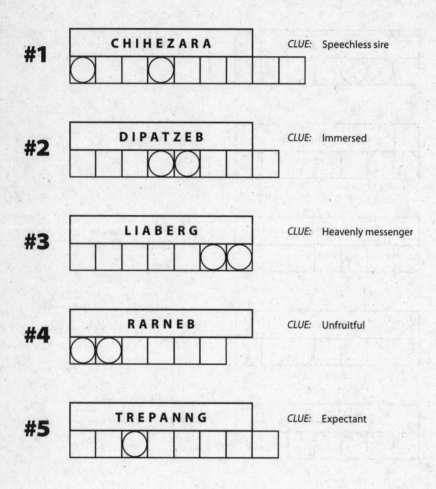

#1 CHIHEZARA   CLUE: Speechless sire

#2 DIPATZEB   CLUE: Immersed

#3 LIABERG   CLUE: Heavenly messenger

#4 RARNEB   CLUE: Unfruitful

#5 TREPANNG   CLUE: Expectant

Arrange the circled letters to solve the mystery person.

MYSTERY ANSWER:

MYSTERY PERSON JUMBLE

Unscramble the Jumbles, one letter to each square, to form words that relate to the mystery person.

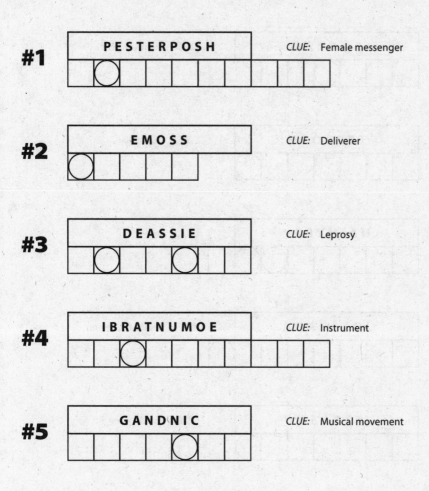

#1 PESTERPOSH

CLUE: Female messenger

#2 EMOSS

CLUE: Deliverer

#3 DEASSIE

CLUE: Leprosy

#4 IBRATNUMOE

CLUE: Instrument

#5 GANDNIC

CLUE: Musical movement

Arrange the circled letters to solve the mystery person.

MYSTERY ANSWER:

MYSTERY PERSON JUMBLE

Unscramble the Jumbles, one letter to each square, to form words that relate to the mystery person.

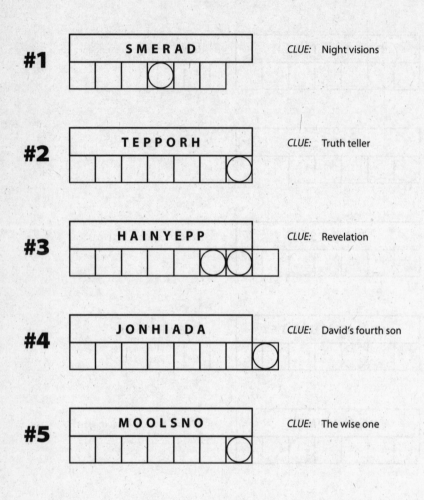

#1 S M E R A D

CLUE: Night visions

#2 T E P P O R H

CLUE: Truth teller

#3 H A I N Y E P P

CLUE: Revelation

#4 J O N H I A D A

CLUE: David's fourth son

#5 M O O L S N O

CLUE: The wise one

Arrange the circled letters to solve the mystery person.

MYSTERY ANSWER:

MYSTERY PERSON JUMBLE

Unscramble the Jumbles, one letter to each square, to form words that relate to the mystery person.

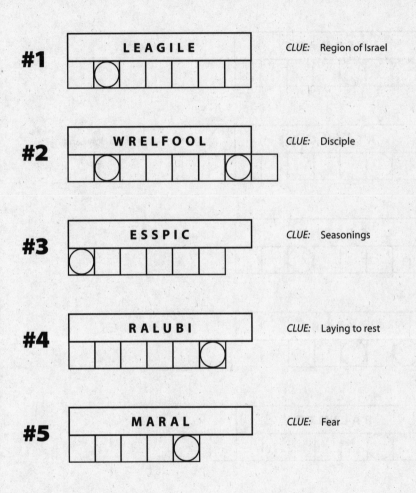

#1 LEAGILE — *CLUE:* Region of Israel

#2 WRELFOOL — *CLUE:* Disciple

#3 ESSPIC — *CLUE:* Seasonings

#4 RALUBI — *CLUE:* Laying to rest

#5 MARAL — *CLUE:* Fear

Arrange the circled letters to solve the mystery person.

MYSTERY ANSWER:

MYSTERY PERSON JUMBLE

Unscramble the Jumbles, one letter to each square, to form words that relate to the mystery person.

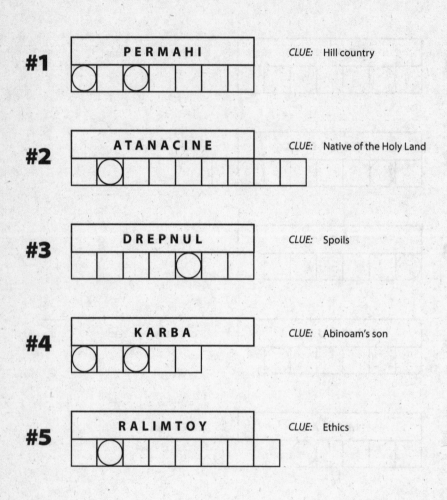

#1 PERMAHI   *CLUE:* Hill country

#2 ATANACINE   *CLUE:* Native of the Holy Land

#3 DREPNUL   *CLUE:* Spoils

#4 KARBA   *CLUE:* Abinoam's son

#5 RALIMTOY   *CLUE:* Ethics

Arrange the circled letters to solve the mystery person.

MYSTERY ANSWER:

MYSTERY PERSON JUMBLE

Unscramble the Jumbles, one letter to each square, to form words that relate to the mystery person.

#1 ZAARSUL *CLUE:* Bethany brother

#2 STESOHS *CLUE:* Woman who entertains

#3 RUERCREST *CLUE:* Bring to life

#4 FROCMOT *CLUE:* Soothe

#5 BYTNEAH *CLUE:* Town near Jerusalem

Arrange the circled letters to solve the mystery person.

MYSTERY ANSWER:

MYSTERY PERSON JUMBLE

Unscramble the Jumbles, one letter to each square, to form words that relate to the mystery person.

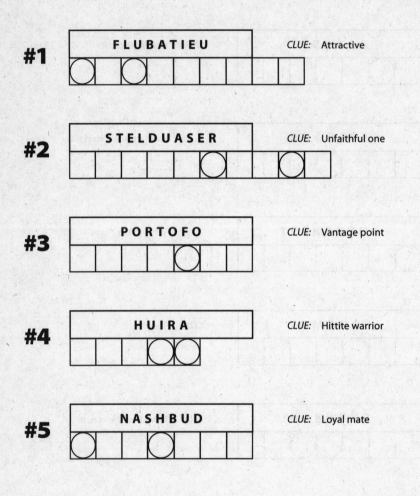

#1 FLUBATIEU   CLUE: Attractive

#2 STELDUASER   CLUE: Unfaithful one

#3 PORTOFO   CLUE: Vantage point

#4 HUIRA   CLUE: Hittite warrior

#5 NASHBUD   CLUE: Loyal mate

Arrange the circled letters to solve the mystery person.

MYSTERY ANSWER:

MYSTERY PERSON JUMBLE

Unscramble the Jumbles, one letter to each square, to form words that relate to the mystery person.

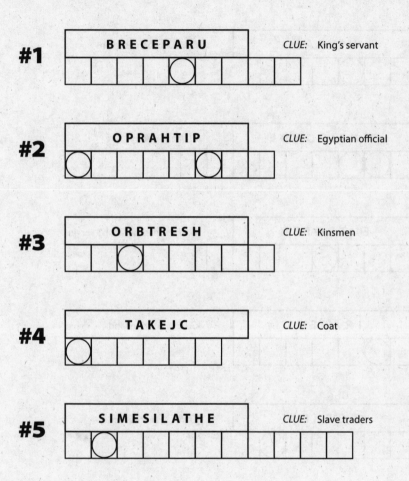

#1 BRECEPARU

CLUE: King's servant

#2 OPRAHTIP

CLUE: Egyptian official

#3 ORBTRESH

CLUE: Kinsmen

#4 TAKEJC

CLUE: Coat

#5 SIMESILATHE

CLUE: Slave traders

Arrange the circled letters to solve the mystery person.

MYSTERY ANSWER:

MYSTERY PERSON JUMBLE

Unscramble the Jumbles, one letter to each square, to form words that relate to the mystery person.

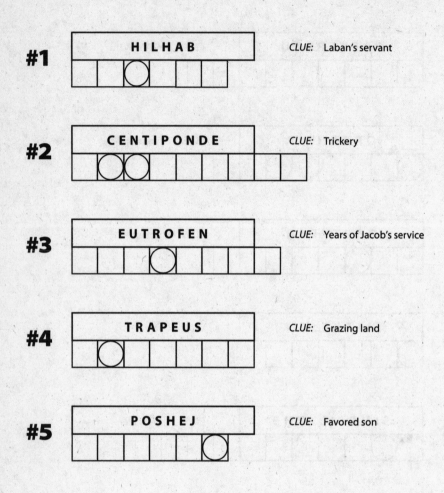

#1   HILHAB   CLUE: Laban's servant

#2   CENTIPONDE   CLUE: Trickery

#3   EUTROFEN   CLUE: Years of Jacob's service

#4   TRAPEUS   CLUE: Grazing land

#5   POSHEJ   CLUE: Favored son

Arrange the circled letters to solve the mystery person.

MYSTERY ANSWER:

MYSTERY PERSON JUMBLE

Unscramble the Jumbles, one letter to each square, to form words that relate to the mystery person.

#1   F U N C A R E   CLUE: Fiery place

#2   N I A N H A H A   CLUE: Friend of Mishael and Azariah

#3   D I N F U E L E D   CLUE: Without blemish

#4   S T R O C U   CLUE: Palace locales

#5   B A N B O Y L   CLUE: Empire

Arrange the circled letters to solve the mystery person.

MYSTERY ANSWER:

MYSTERY PERSON JUMBLE

Unscramble the Jumbles, one letter to each square, to form words that relate to the mystery person.

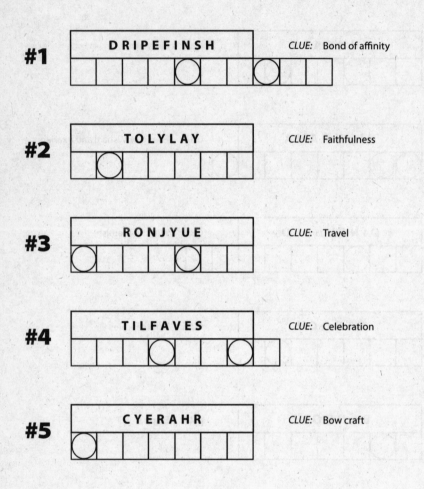

#1 DRIPEFINSH

CLUE: Bond of affinity

#2 TOLYLAY

CLUE: Faithfulness

#3 RONJYUE

CLUE: Travel

#4 TILFAVES

CLUE: Celebration

#5 CYERAHR

CLUE: Bow craft

Arrange the circled letters to solve the mystery person.

MYSTERY ANSWER:

MYSTERY PERSON JUMBLE

Unscramble the Jumbles, one letter to each square, to form words that relate to the mystery person.

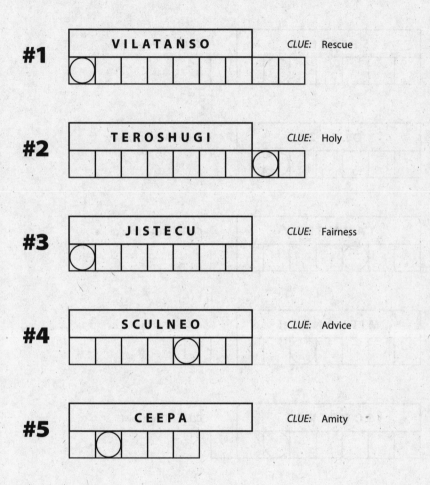

#1 VILATANSO

CLUE: Rescue

#2 TEROSHUGI

CLUE: Holy

#3 JISTECU

CLUE: Fairness

#4 SCULNEO

CLUE: Advice

#5 CEEPA

CLUE: Amity

Arrange the circled letters to solve the mystery person.

MYSTERY ANSWER:

MYSTERY PERSON JUMBLE

Unscramble the Jumbles, one letter to each square, to form words that relate to the mystery person.

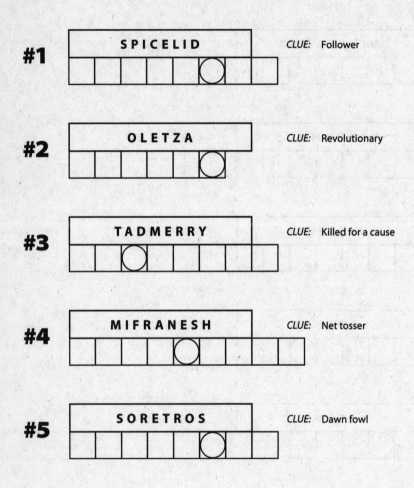

#1 SPICELID

CLUE: Follower

#2 OLETZA

CLUE: Revolutionary

#3 TADMERRY

CLUE: Killed for a cause

#4 MIFRANESH

CLUE: Net tosser

#5 SORETROS

CLUE: Dawn fowl

Arrange the circled letters to solve the mystery person.

MYSTERY ANSWER:

MYSTERY PERSON JUMBLE

Unscramble the Jumbles, one letter to each square, to form words that relate to the mystery person.

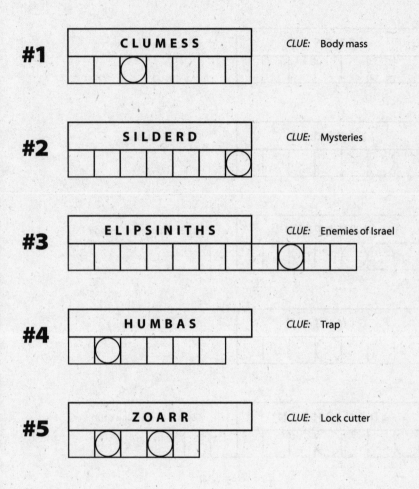

#1 CLUMESS   CLUE: Body mass

#2 SILDERD   CLUE: Mysteries

#3 ELIPSINITHS   CLUE: Enemies of Israel

#4 HUMBAS   CLUE: Trap

#5 ZOARR   CLUE: Lock cutter

Arrange the circled letters to solve the mystery person.

MYSTERY ANSWER:

MYSTERY PERSON JUMBLE

Unscramble the Jumbles, one letter to each square, to form words that relate to the mystery person.

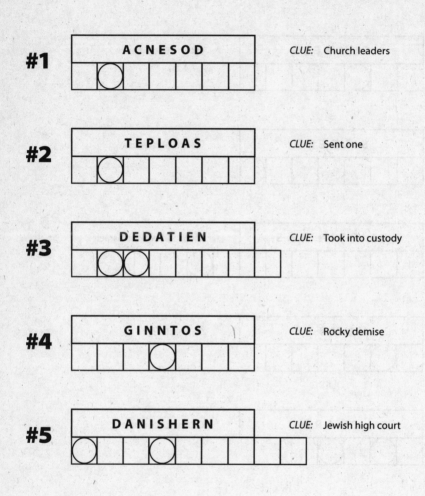

#1 ACNESOD — CLUE: Church leaders

#2 TEPLOAS — CLUE: Sent one

#3 DEDATIEN — CLUE: Took into custody

#4 GINNTOS — CLUE: Rocky demise

#5 DANISHERN — CLUE: Jewish high court

Arrange the circled letters to solve the mystery person.

MYSTERY ANSWER:

MYSTERY PERSON JUMBLE

Unscramble the Jumbles, one letter to each square, to form words that relate to the mystery person.

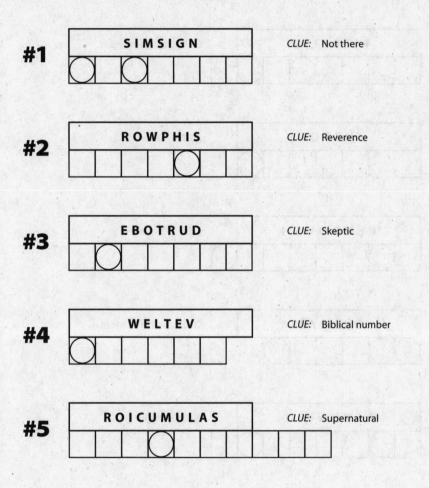

#1 SIMSIGN

CLUE: Not there

#2 ROWPHIS

CLUE: Reverence

#3 EBOTRUD

CLUE: Skeptic

#4 WELTEV

CLUE: Biblical number

#5 ROICUMULAS

CLUE: Supernatural

Arrange the circled letters to solve the mystery person.

MYSTERY ANSWER:

MYSTERY PERSON JUMBLE

Unscramble the Jumbles, one letter to each square, to form words that relate to the mystery person.

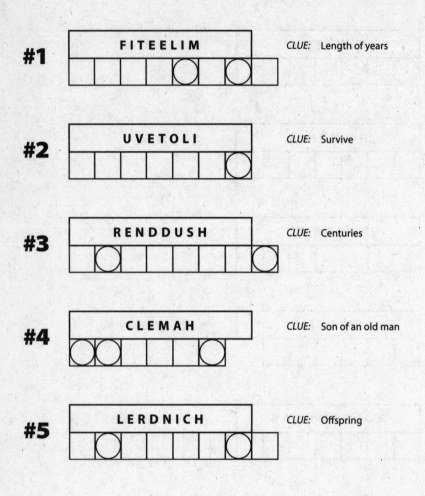

#1 FITEELIM   CLUE: Length of years

#2 UVETOLI   CLUE: Survive

#3 RENDDUSH   CLUE: Centuries

#4 CLEMAH   CLUE: Son of an old man

#5 LERDNICH   CLUE: Offspring

Arrange the circled letters to solve the mystery person.

MYSTERY ANSWER:

MYSTERY PERSON JUMBLE

Unscramble the Jumbles, one letter to each square, to form words that relate to the mystery person.

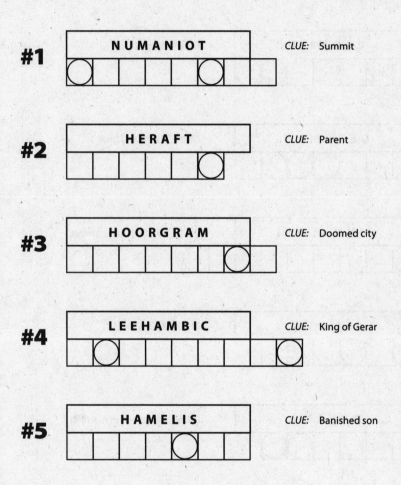

#1 NUMANIOT CLUE: Summit

#2 HERAFT CLUE: Parent

#3 HOORGRAM CLUE: Doomed city

#4 LEEHAMBIC CLUE: King of Gerar

#5 HAMELIS CLUE: Banished son

Arrange the circled letters to solve the mystery person.

MYSTERY ANSWER:

MYSTERY PERSON JUMBLE

Unscramble the Jumbles, one letter to each square, to form words that relate to the mystery person.

#1 CARMILE   CLUE: Marvel

#2 DEROMUN   CLUE: Expressed grief

#3 GINNATONI   CLUE: Used perfume for this

#4 SEMDON   CLUE: Spirits

#5 DUSANY   CLUE: Resurrection morning

Arrange the circled letters to solve the mystery person.

MYSTERY ANSWER:

MYSTERY PERSON JUMBLE

Unscramble the Jumbles, one letter to each square, to form words that relate to the mystery person.

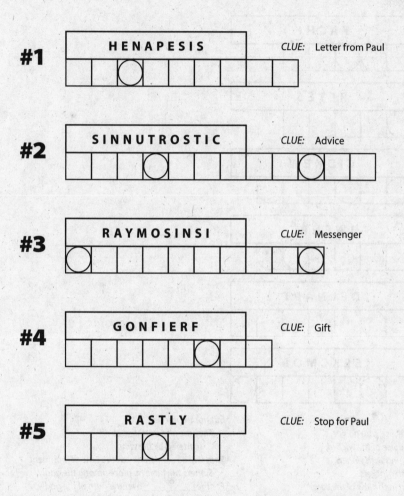

#1 HENAPESIS CLUE: Letter from Paul

#2 SINNUTROSTIC CLUE: Advice

#3 RAYMOSINSI CLUE: Messenger

#4 GONFIERF CLUE: Gift

#5 RASTLY CLUE: Stop for Paul

Arrange the circled letters to solve the mystery person.

MYSTERY ANSWER:

PSALM JUMBLE

See if you can unscramble the letters to form the words without looking at the psalm first. If you get stumped, look for the answers in the psalm. Then arrange the circled letters to solve the Mystery Answer, below, suggested by the Jumble words.

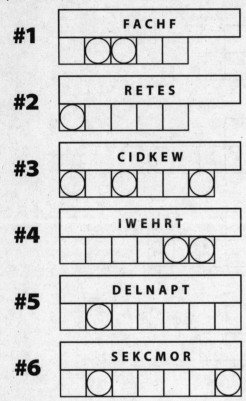

#1 FACHF

#2 RETES

#3 CIDKEW

#4 IWEHRT

#5 DELNAPT

#6 SEKCMOR

Psalm 1:1-6

[1] Oh, the joys of those who do not
   follow the advice of the wicked,
   or stand around with sinners,
   or join in with mockers.
[2] But they delight in the law of the Lord,
   meditating on it day and night.
[3] They are like trees planted along the riverbank,
   bearing fruit each season.
   Their leaves never wither,
   and they prosper in all they do.

[4] But not the wicked!
   They are like worthless chaff,
      scattered by the wind.
[5] They will be condemned at the time of judgment.
   Sinners will have no place among the godly.
[6] For the _____ over the path of the godly,
   but the path of the wicked leads to destruction.

MYSTERY ANSWER:

PSALM JUMBLE

See if you can unscramble the letters to form the words without looking at the psalm first. If you get stumped, look for the answers in the psalm. Then arrange the circled letters to solve the Mystery Answer, below, suggested by the Jumble words.

#1 LAYVEL

#2 LESCO

#3 SOGOSDEN

#4 PEDRHESH

#5 NIFGUNALI

#6 WERLOVSOF

Psalm 23:1-6

[1] The LORD is my shepherd;
   I have all that I need.
[2] He lets me rest in green meadows;
   he leads me beside _____ streams.
[3]   He renews my strength.
 He guides me along right paths,
   bringing honor to his name.
[4] Even when I walk
   through the darkest valley,
 I will not be afraid,

for you are close beside me.
Your rod and your staff
   protect and comfort me.
[5] You prepare a feast for me
   in the presence of my enemies.
 You honor me by anointing my head with oil.
   My cup overflows with blessings.
[6] Surely your goodness and unfailing love will
   pursue me
   all the days of my life,
 and I will live in the house of the LORD forever.

MYSTERY ANSWER:

PSALM JUMBLE

See if you can unscramble the letters to form the words without looking at the psalm first. If you get stumped, look for the answers in the psalm. Then arrange the circled letters to solve the Mystery Answer, below, suggested by the Jumble words.

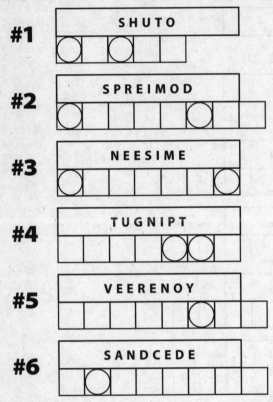

#1 SHUTO

#2 SPREIMOD

#3 NEESIME

#4 TUGNIPT

#5 VEERENOY

#6 SANDCEDE

Psalm 47:1-6

[1] Come, everyone! Clap your hands!
   Shout to God with joyful praise!
[2] For the LORD Most High is awesome.
   He is the great King of all the earth.
[3] He subdues the nations before us,
   putting our enemies beneath our feet.
[4] He chose the Promised Land as our inheritance,
   the proud _____ of Jacob's descendants,
   whom he loves.

[5] God has ascended with a mighty shout.
   The LORD has ascended with trumpets blaring.
[6] Sing praises to God, sing praises;
   sing praises to our King, sing praises!

MYSTERY ANSWER:

PSALM JUMBLE

See if you can unscramble the letters to form the words without looking at the psalm first. If you get stumped, look for the answers in the psalm. Then arrange the circled letters to solve the Mystery Answer, below, suggested by the Jumble words.

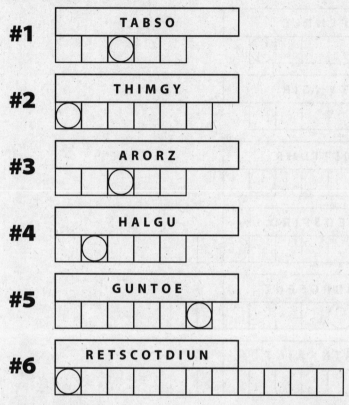

#1 TABSO

#2 THIMGY

#3 ARORZ

#4 HALGU

#5 GUNTOE

#6 RETSCOTDIUN

Psalm 52:1-2, 5-7, 9

¹ Why do you boast about your crimes, great warrior?
  Don't you realize God's justice continues forever?
² All day long you plot destruction.
  Your tongue cuts like a sharp razor;
  you're an expert at telling lies. . . .
⁵ But God will strike you down once and for all.
  He will pull you from your home
  and uproot you from the land of the living.
⁶ The righteous will see it and be _____.
  They will laugh and say,

⁷ "Look what happens to mighty warriors
  who do not trust in God.
  They trust their wealth instead
  and grow more and more bold in their
    wickedness." . . .
⁹ I will praise you forever, O God,
  for what you have done.
  I will trust in your good name
  in the presence of your faithful people.

MYSTERY ANSWER:

79

PSALM JUMBLE

See if you can unscramble the letters to form the words without looking at the psalm first. If you get stumped, look for the answers in the psalm. Then arrange the circled letters to solve the Mystery Answer, below, suggested by the Jumble words.

#1 PEHRLE

#2 TYNGIR

#3 MIPTUHR

#4 MEDSPIRO

#5 SARRGSENT

#6 CATNKAIGT

Psalm 54:2-7

[2] Listen to my _____, O God.
Pay attention to my plea.
[3] For strangers are attacking me;
violent people are trying to kill me.
They care nothing for God.
[4] But God is my helper.
The Lord keeps me alive!
[5] May the evil plans of my enemies be turned against
them.
Do as you promised and put an end to them.

[6] I will sacrifice a voluntary offering to you;
I will praise your name, O LORD,
for it is good.
[7] For you have rescued me from my troubles
and helped me to triumph over my enemies.

MYSTERY ANSWER:

PSALM JUMBLE

See if you can unscramble the letters to form the words without looking at the psalm first. If you get stumped, look for the answers in the psalm. Then arrange the circled letters to solve the Mystery Answer, below, suggested by the Jumble words.

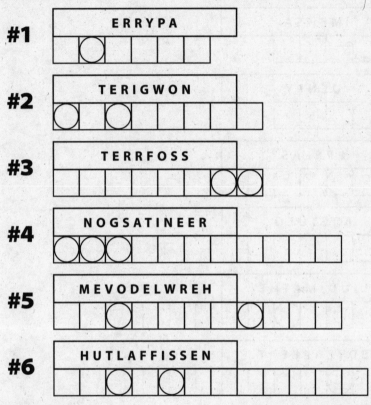

#1 ERRYPA

#2 TERIGWON

#3 TERRFOSS

#4 NOGSATINEER

#5 MEVODELWREH

#6 HUTLAFFISSEN

Psalm 61:1-4, 6-7

1 O God, listen to my cry!
   Hear my prayer!
2 From the ends of the earth,
   I cry to you for help
   when my heart is overwhelmed.
   Lead me to the towering rock of safety,
3   for you are my safe refuge,
   a fortress where my enemies cannot reach me.
4 Let me live forever in your sanctuary,
   safe beneath the _____! . . .

6 Add many years to the life of the king!
   May his years span the generations!
7 May he reign under God's protection forever.
   May your unfailing love and faithfulness watch
   over him.

MYSTERY ANSWER:

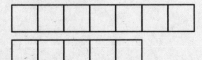 OF YOUR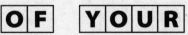

81

PSALM JUMBLE

See if you can unscramble the letters to form the words without looking at the psalm first. If you get stumped, look for the answers in the psalm. Then arrange the circled letters to solve the Mystery Answer, below, suggested by the Jumble words.

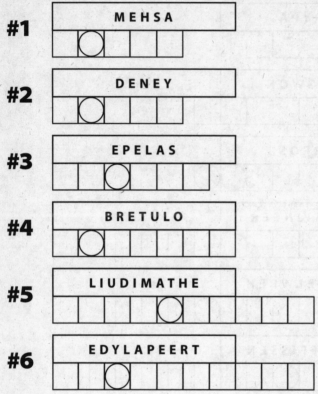

#1 MEHSA

#2 DENEY

#3 EPELAS

#4 BRETULO

#5 LIUDIMATHE

#6 EDYLAPEERT

Psalm 70:1-5

[1] Please, God, rescue me!
  Come quickly, LORD, and help me.
[2] May those who try to kill me
  be humiliated and put to shame.
May those who take delight in my trouble
  be turned back in disgrace.
[3] Let them be horrified by their shame,
  for they said, "Aha! We've got him now!"
[4] But may all who search for you
  be filled with joy and gladness in you.

May those who love your salvation
  repeatedly shout, "God is great!"
[5] But as for me, I am poor and needy;
  please hurry to my aid, O God.
You are my _____ and my savior;
  O LORD, do not delay.

MYSTERY ANSWER:

82

PSALM JUMBLE

See if you can unscramble the letters to form the words without looking at the psalm first. If you get stumped, look for the answers in the psalm. Then arrange the circled letters to solve the Mystery Answer, below, suggested by the Jumble words.

#1 BOATU

#2 EANHELVY

#3 ONGATRIN

#4 PODSEPERS

#5 ETTUSTIED

#6 COOSRUNNEP

Psalm 82:1-5, 8

[1] God presides over heaven's court;
   he pronounces judgment on the heavenly beings:
[2] "How long will you hand down unjust decisions
   by favoring the wicked?
[3] "Give justice to the poor and the orphan;
   uphold the rights of the oppressed and the
      destitute.
[4] Rescue the poor and helpless;
   deliver them from the grasp of evil people.
[5] But these oppressors know nothing;

   they are so ignorant!
They wander about in darkness,
   while the whole world is shaken to the core....
[8] Rise up, O God, and judge the earth,
   for all the _____ to you.

MYSTERY ANSWER:

83

PSALM JUMBLE

See if you can unscramble the letters to form the words without looking at the psalm first. If you get stumped, look for the answers in the psalm. Then arrange the circled letters to solve the Mystery Answer, below, suggested by the Jumble words.

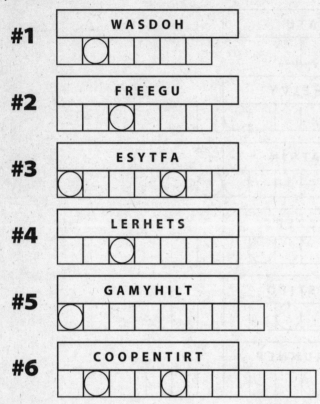

#1 WASDOH

#2 FREEGU

#3 ESYTFA

#4 LERHETS

#5 GAMYHILT

#6 COOPENTIRT

Psalm 91:1-7

¹ Those who live in the shelter of the Most High
   will find rest in the shadow of the Almighty.
² This I declare about the LORD:
   He alone is my refuge, my place of safety;
   he is my God, and I trust him.
³ For he will rescue you from every trap
   and protect you from deadly disease.
⁴ He will cover you with his _____.
   He will shelter you with his wings.

His faithful promises are your armor and
   protection.
⁵ Do not be afraid of the terrors of the night,
   nor the arrow that flies in the day.
⁶ Do not dread the disease that stalks in darkness,
   nor the disaster that strikes at midday.
⁷ Though a thousand fall at your side,
   though ten thousand are dying around you,
   these evils will not touch you.

MYSTERY ANSWER:

PSALM JUMBLE

See if you can unscramble the letters to form the words without looking at the psalm first. If you get stumped, look for the answers in the psalm. Then arrange the circled letters to solve the Mystery Answer, below, suggested by the Jumble words.

#1 ROWPE

#2 FLOUJY

#3 TRICVOY

#4 DORLUFWEN

#5 BREEDEREMM

#6 SEESTRONGISHU

Psalm 98:1-6

¹ Sing a new song to the LORD,
   for he has done wonderful deeds.
His right hand has won a mighty victory;
   his holy arm has shown his saving power!
² The LORD has announced his victory
   and has revealed his righteousness to every
      nation!
³ He has remembered his promise to love and be
   faithful to Israel.

The ends of the earth have seen the victory
   of our God.
⁴ Shout to the LORD, all the earth;
   break out in praise and sing for joy!
⁵ Sing your praise to the LORD with the harp,
   with the harp and melodious song,
⁶ with trumpets and the sound of the ram's horn.
   Make a joyful _____ before the LORD, the
   King!

MYSTERY ANSWER:

85

PSALM JUMBLE

See if you can unscramble the letters to form the words without looking at the psalm first. If you get stumped, look for the answers in the psalm. Then arrange the circled letters to solve the Mystery Answer, below, suggested by the Jumble words.

#1 TEPSURA

#2 PRIWOSH

#3 SELSDNAG

#4 NAITGRENOE

#5 GOWNCADELEK

#6 KINGHASNTGIV

Psalm 100:1-5

1 Shout with joy to the LORD, all the earth!
2 Worship the LORD with gladness.
Come before him, singing with joy.
3 Acknowledge that the LORD is God!
He made us, and we are his.
We are his people, the sheep of his pasture.
4 Enter his gates with thanksgiving;
go into his courts with praise.
Give thanks to him and praise his name.

5 For the LORD is good.
His unfailing _____ forever,
and his faithfulness continues to each generation.

MYSTERY ANSWER:

PSALM JUMBLE

See if you can unscramble the letters to form the words without looking at the psalm first. If you get stumped, look for the answers in the psalm. Then arrange the circled letters to solve the Mystery Answer, below, suggested by the Jumble words.

#1 NOROH

#2 TOLOFOTSO

#3 DETNEX

#4 DEARRAY

#5 GLIWLYINL

#6 LIKEDMCHEEZ

Psalm 110:1-5

[1] The Lord said to my Lord,
  "Sit in the place of honor at my _____
until I humble your enemies,
  making them a footstool under your feet."
[2] The Lord will extend your powerful kingdom from
    Jerusalem;
  you will rule over your enemies.
[3] When you go to war,
  your people will serve you willingly.
  You are arrayed in holy garments,

and your strength will be renewed each day like
    the morning dew.
[4] The Lord has taken an oath and will not break his
    vow:
  "You are a priest forever in the order of
    Melchizedek."
[5] The Lord stands at your right hand to protect you.

MYSTERY ANSWER:

PSALM JUMBLE

See if you can unscramble the letters to form the words without looking at the psalm first. If you get stumped, look for the answers in the psalm. Then arrange the circled letters to solve the Mystery Answer, below, suggested by the Jumble words.

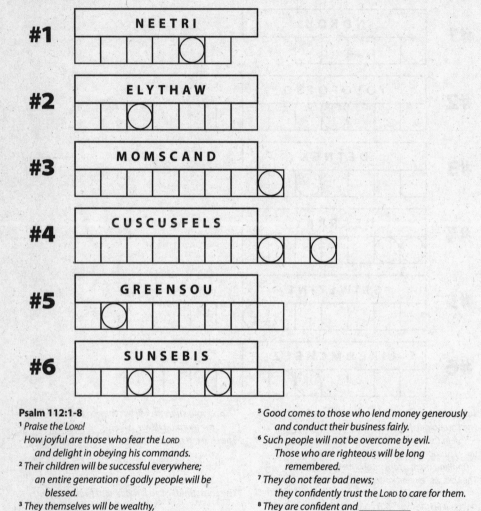

#1 NEETRI

#2 ELYTHAW

#3 MOMSCAND

#4 CUSCUSFELS

#5 GREENSOU

#6 SUNSEBIS

Psalm 112:1-8

[1] Praise the LORD!
 How joyful are those who fear the LORD
  and delight in obeying his commands.
[2] Their children will be successful everywhere;
  an entire generation of godly people will be
   blessed.
[3] They themselves will be wealthy,
  and their good deeds will last forever.
[4] Light shines in the darkness for the godly.
  They are generous, compassionate, and righteous.

[5] Good comes to those who lend money generously
  and conduct their business fairly.
[6] Such people will not be overcome by evil.
  Those who are righteous will be long
   remembered.
[7] They do not fear bad news;
  they confidently trust the LORD to care for them.
[8] They are confident and _____
  and can face their foes triumphantly.

MYSTERY ANSWER:

88

PSALM JUMBLE

See if you can unscramble the letters to form the words without looking at the psalm first. If you get stumped, look for the answers in the psalm. Then arrange the circled letters to solve the Mystery Answer, below, suggested by the Jumble words.

#1 NAGAI

#2 CATPEC

#3 CANLABE

#4 RIPEMOS

#5 GETSHOIRU

#6 ERNMEEDDIT

Psalm 119:105-112

105 Your word is a lamp to guide my feet
      and a light for my path.
106 I've promised it once, and I'll promise it again:
      I will obey your righteous regulations.
107 I have suffered much, O LORD;
      restore my life again as you promised.
108 LORD, accept my offering of praise,
      and teach me your regulations.
109 My life constantly hangs in the balance,
      but I will not stop obeying your _____.

110 The wicked have set their traps for me,
      but I will not turn from your commandments.
111 Your laws are my treasure;
      they are my heart's delight.
112 I am determined to keep your decrees
      to the very end.

MYSTERY ANSWER:

89

PSALM JUMBLE

See if you can unscramble the letters to form the words without looking at the psalm first. If you get stumped, look for the answers in the psalm. Then arrange the circled letters to solve the Mystery Answer, below, suggested by the Jumble words.

#1 SEDIEB

#2 AHNEVE

#3 HIFSLEM

#4 AUMINNOTS

#5 BUSMERLS

#6 OPTICVRETE

Psalm 121:1-8

[1] I look up to the mountains—
   does my help come from there?
[2] My help comes from the Lord,
   who made heaven and earth!
[3] He will not let you stumble;
   the one who watches over you will not slumber.
[4] Indeed, he who watches over Israel
   never slumbers or sleeps.

[5] The Lord himself watches over you!
   The Lord stands beside you as your protective
   shade.
[6] The sun will not harm you by day,
   nor the moon at night.
[7] The Lord keeps you from all harm
   and watches over your life.
[8] The Lord keeps watch over you as you come and go,
   both now and _____.

MYSTERY ANSWER:

PSALM JUMBLE

See if you can unscramble the letters to form the words without looking at the psalm first. If you get stumped, look for the answers in the psalm. Then arrange the circled letters to solve the Mystery Answer, below, suggested by the Jumble words.

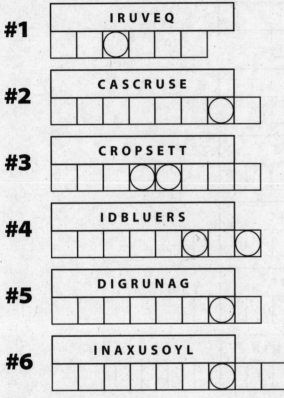

#1 IRUVEQ

#2 CASCRUSE

#3 CROPSETT

#4 IDBLUERS

#5 DIGRUNAG

#6 INAXUSOYL

Psalm 127:1-5

¹ Unless the Lᴏʀᴅ builds a house,
   the work of the builders is wasted.
Unless the Lᴏʀᴅ protects a city,
   guarding it with _____ will do no good.
² It is useless for you to work so hard
   from early morning until late at night,
anxiously working for food to eat;
   for God gives rest to his loved ones.
³ Children are a gift from the Lᴏʀᴅ;
   they are a reward from him.

⁴ Children born to a young man
   are like arrows in a warrior's hands.
⁵ How joyful is the man whose quiver is full of them!
   He will not be put to shame when he confronts his
   accusers at the city gates.

MYSTERY ANSWER:

PSALM JUMBLE

See if you can unscramble the letters to form the words without looking at the psalm first. If you get stumped, look for the answers in the psalm. Then arrange the circled letters to solve the Mystery Answer, below, suggested by the Jumble words.

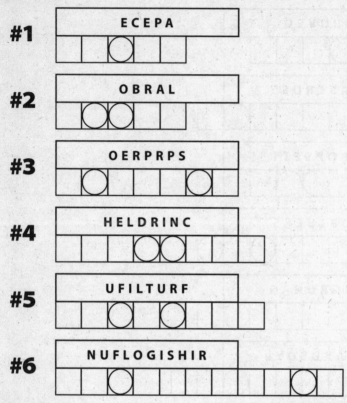

#1 ECEPA

#2 OBRAL

#3 OERPRPS

#4 HELDRINC

#5 UFILTURF

#6 NUFLOGISHIR

Psalm 128:1-6

1 How joyful are those who fear the Lord—
   all who follow his ways!
2 You will enjoy the fruit of your labor.
   How joyful and prosperous you will be!
3 Your wife will be like a fruitful grapevine,
   flourishing within your home.
Your children will be like vigorous young olive trees
   as they sit _____.
4 That is the Lord's blessing
   for those who fear him.

5 May the Lord continually bless you from Zion.
   May you see Jerusalem prosper as long as you live.
6 May you live to enjoy your grandchildren.
   May Israel have peace!

MYSTERY ANSWER:

☐☐☐☐☐☐ **YOUR** ☐☐☐☐☐

PSALM JUMBLE

See if you can unscramble the letters to form the words without looking at the psalm first. If you get stumped, look for the answers in the psalm. Then arrange the circled letters to solve the Mystery Answer, below, suggested by the Jumble words.

#1 FEERUS

#2 UHOYT

#3 NEEMSIE

#4 LEPWOD

#5 NUGOYLD

#6 VECEDOR

Psalm 129:1-4, 8

[1] From my earliest youth my enemies have
_____ me.
    Let all Israel repeat this:
[2] From my earliest youth my enemies have persecuted me,
    but they have never defeated me.
[3] My back is covered with cuts,
    as if a farmer had plowed long furrows.

[4] But the LORD is good;
    he has cut me free from the ropes of the ungodly....
[8] And may those who pass by
    refuse to give them this blessing:
    "The LORD bless you;
    we bless you in the LORD's name."

MYSTERY ANSWER:

93

PSALM JUMBLE

See if you can unscramble the letters to form the words without looking at the psalm first. If you get stumped, look for the answers in the psalm. Then arrange the circled letters to solve the Mystery Answer, below, suggested by the Jumble words.

#1 MEREDE

#2 FLEMISH

#3 RUSVIEV

#4 GOINNUCT

#5 TANENTOIT

#6 WOVSOFREL

Psalm 130:1-5, 7-8

[1] From the depths of despair, O Lord,
    I call for your help.
[2] Hear my cry, O Lord.
    Pay attention to my prayer.
[3] Lord, if you kept a record of our sins,
    who, O Lord, could ever survive?
[4] But you offer _____,
    that we might learn to fear you.

[5] I am counting on the Lord;
    yes, I am counting on him.
    I have put my hope in his word. . . .
[7] O Israel, hope in the Lord;
    for with the Lord there is unfailing love.
    His redemption overflows.
[8] He himself will redeem Israel
    from every kind of sin.

MYSTERY ANSWER:

PSALM JUMBLE

See if you can unscramble the letters to form the words without looking at the psalm first. If you get stumped, look for the answers in the psalm. Then arrange the circled letters to solve the Mystery Answer, below, suggested by the Jumble words.

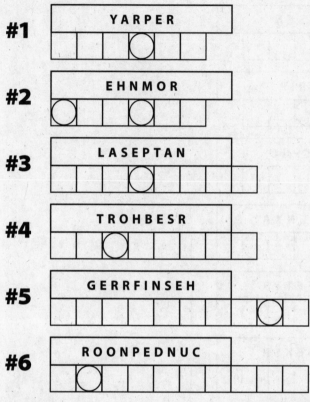

#1 YARPER

#2 EHNMOR

#3 LASEPTAN

#4 TROHBESR

#5 GERRFINSEH

#6 ROONPEDNUC

Psalm 133:1, 3

[1] How wonderful and pleasant it is
   when brothers live together in _____!...

[3] Harmony is as refreshing as the dew from Mount Hermon
   that falls on the mountains of Zion.
   And there the LORD has pronounced his blessing,
   even life everlasting.

Psalm 134:1-3

[1] Oh, praise the LORD, all you servants of the LORD,
   you who serve at night in the house of the LORD.

[2] Lift up holy hands in prayer,
   and praise the LORD.

[3] May the LORD, who made heaven and earth,
   bless you from Jerusalem.

MYSTERY ANSWER:

95

PSALM JUMBLE

See if you can unscramble the letters to form the words without looking at the psalm first. If you get stumped, look for the answers in the psalm. Then arrange the circled letters to solve the Mystery Answer, below, suggested by the Jumble words.

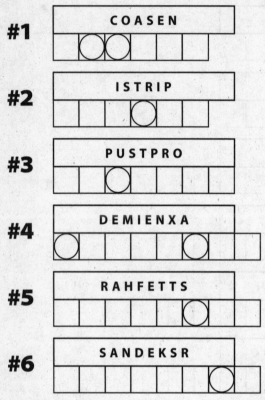

#1 COASEN

#2 ISTRIP

#3 PUSTPRO

#4 DEMIENXA

#5 RAHFETTS

#6 SANDEKSR

Psalm 139:1-2, 7-12

1 O Lord, you have examined my heart
    and know everything about me.
2 You know when I sit down or stand up.
    You know my thoughts even when I'm far away. . . .
7 I can never escape from your Spirit!
    I can never get away from your _____!
8 If I go up to heaven, you are there;
    if I go down to the grave, you are there.
9 If I ride the wings of the morning,
    if I dwell by the farthest oceans,

10 even there your hand will guide me,
    and your strength will support me.
11 I could ask the darkness to hide me
    and the light around me to become night—
12 but even in darkness I cannot hide from you.
    To you the night shines as bright as day.
    Darkness and light are the same to you.

MYSTERY ANSWER:

PSALM JUMBLE

See if you can unscramble the letters to form the words without looking at the psalm first. If you get stumped, look for the answers in the psalm. Then arrange the circled letters to solve the Mystery Answer, below, suggested by the Jumble words.

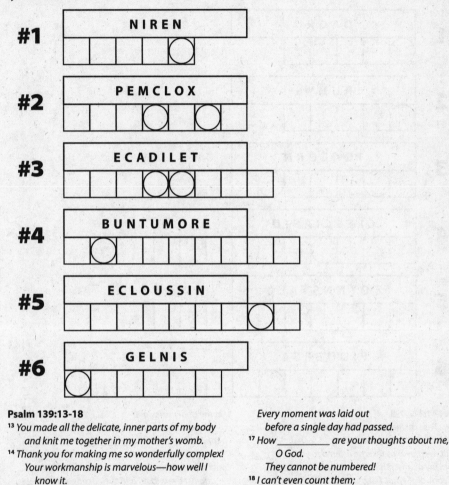

#1 NIREN

#2 PEMCLOX

#3 ECADILET

#4 BUNTUMORE

#5 ECLOUSSIN

#6 GELNIS

Psalm 139:13-18

13 You made all the delicate, inner parts of my body
   and knit me together in my mother's womb.
14 Thank you for making me so wonderfully complex!
   Your workmanship is marvelous—how well I
      know it.
15 You watched me as I was being formed in utter
      seclusion,
   as I was woven together in the dark of the womb.
16 You saw me before I was born.
   Every day of my life was recorded in your book.

Every moment was laid out
   before a single day had passed.
17 How _____ are your thoughts about me,
      O God.
   They cannot be numbered!
18 I can't even count them;
   they outnumber the grains of sand!
And when I wake up,
   you are still with me!

MYSTERY ANSWER:

97

PSALM JUMBLE

See if you can unscramble the letters to form the words without looking at the psalm first. If you get stumped, look for the answers in the psalm. Then arrange the circled letters to solve the Mystery Answer, below, suggested by the Jumble words.

#1 D A G R U

#2 R U H Y R

#3 T O C L O R N

#4 C L E E C I A S I D

#5 T O Y N N S T A L C

#6 P I D U E R S A

Psalm 141:1-5, 7-8

[1] O Lord, I am calling to you. Please hurry!
 Listen when I cry to you for help!
[2] Accept my prayer as incense offered to you,
 and my upraised hands as an evening offering.
[3] Take control of what I say, O Lord,
 and guard my lips.
[4] Don't let me drift toward evil
 or take part in acts of wickedness.
 Don't let me share in the delicacies
 of those who do wrong.

[5] Let the godly strike me!
 It will be a kindness!
 If they correct me, it is _____ medicine.
 Don't let me refuse it.
 But I pray constantly
 against the wicked and their deeds....
[7] Like rocks brought up by a plow,
 the bones of the wicked will lie scattered
 without burial.
[8] I look to you for help, O Sovereign Lord.
 You are my refuge; don't let them kill me.

MYSTERY ANSWER:

98

PSALM JUMBLE

See if you can unscramble the letters to form the words without looking at the psalm first. If you get stumped, look for the answers in the psalm. Then arrange the circled letters to solve the Mystery Answer, below, suggested by the Jumble words.

#1 ENDOBY

#2 HASKNT

#3 BAOUSLET

#4 BLENRUGIDI

#5 HELFIGULDT

#6 SIPREAS

Psalm 147:1-5, 7

[1] Praise the LORD!
   How good to sing praises to our God!
      How delightful and how fitting!
[2] The LORD is rebuilding Jerusalem
      and bringing the exiles back to Israel.
[3] He heals the _____
      and bandages their wounds.
[4] He counts the stars
      and calls them all by name.

[5] How great is our Lord! His power is absolute!
      His understanding is beyond comprehension! . . .
[7] Sing out your thanks to the LORD;
      sing praises to our God with a harp.

MYSTERY ANSWER:

PSALM JUMBLE

See if you can unscramble the letters to form the words without looking at the psalm first. If you get stumped, look for the answers in the psalm. Then arrange the circled letters to solve the Mystery Answer, below, suggested by the Jumble words.

#1 SABERTEH

#2 TREGESSAN

#3 CLAMBSY

#4 BOATURIMEN

#5 GADNNIC

#6 TINVEREGHY

Psalm 150:1-6

[1] *Praise the LORD!*
   Praise God in his _____;
      praise him in his mighty heaven!
[2] *Praise him for his mighty works;*
      praise his unequaled greatness!
[3] *Praise him with a blast of the ram's horn;*
      praise him with the lyre and harp!
[4] *Praise him with the tambourine and dancing;*
      praise him with strings and flutes!

[5] *Praise him with a clash of cymbals;*
      praise him with loud clanging cymbals.
[6] *Let everything that breathes sing praises to the LORD!*
   Praise the LORD!

MYSTERY ANSWER:

WHO SAID THAT? JUMBLE

Using the quotes below as clues, try to unscramble the mixed-up letters to form the names of the people responsible for the quotes.

#1 "Well, aren't you going to answer these charges? What do you have to say for yourself?"

GRISHEHPIT

#2 "How can I be sure this will happen? I'm an old man now, and my wife is also well along in years."

CHERHAZIA

#3 "How kind the Lord is! He has taken away my disgrace of having no children."

ZILATBEEH

#4 "Glory to God in highest heaven, and peace on earth to those with whom God is pleased."

SLENAG

#5 "Rabbi, you are the Son of God—the King of Israel!"

HANALANTE

#6 "Is it legal to convict a man before he is given a hearing?"

MOCNEDSUI

WHO SAID THAT? JUMBLE

Using the quotes below as clues, try to unscramble the mixed-up letters to form the names of the people responsible for the quotes.

#1 "Why does your teacher eat with such scum?"

SHERIEPSA

#2 "Are you the Messiah we've been expecting, or should we keep looking for someone else?"

DHISSSONCLIPEJ

#3 "Leave that innocent man alone. I suffered through a terrible nightmare about him last night."

WITLEFASIPE

#4 "Ask for the head of John the Baptist!"

SARDOIHE

#5 "Teacher, Moses gave us a law that if a man dies, leaving a wife but no children, his brother should marry the widow and have a child who will carry on the brother's name."

DUCSESEDA

#6 "Rejoice in the Lord always. I will say it again: Rejoice! Let your gentleness be evident to all. The Lord is near."

LAUTLEPASPO

WHO SAID THAT? JUMBLE

Using the quotes below as clues, try to unscramble the mixed-up letters to form the names of the people responsible for the quotes.

#1 "They left the town at dusk, as the gates were about to close. I don't know where they went. If you hurry, you can probably catch up with them."

BRAHA

#2 "Today we know the LORD is among us because you have not committed this treachery against the LORD as we thought. Instead, you have rescued Israel from being destroyed by the hand of the LORD."

HESIHNAP

#3 "Let me have another gift. You have already given me land in the Negev; now please give me springs of water, too."

SHACA

#4 "Very well, I will go with you. But you will receive no honor in this venture, for the LORD's victory over Sisera will be at the hands of a woman."

ROBHADE

#5 "Get up! For the LORD has given you victory over the Midianite hordes!"

NEIDOG

#6 "Listen to me, citizens of Shechem! Listen to me if you want God to listen to you! Once upon a time the trees decided to choose a king. First they said to the olive tree, 'Be our king!'"

MOTHJA

103

WHO SAID THAT? JUMBLE

Using the quotes below as clues, try to unscramble the mixed-up letters to form the names of the people responsible for the quotes.

#1 "Hear, O Israel: The LORD our God, the LORD is one. Love the LORD your God with all your heart and with all your soul and with all your strength."

EMOSS

#2 "Destroy the idols among you, and turn your hearts to the LORD, the God of Israel."

HAJUSO

#3 "Who am I, O Sovereign LORD, and what is my family, that you have brought me this far?"

DADGINVIK

#4 "I will give half my wealth to the poor, Lord, and if I have cheated people on their taxes, I will give them back four times as much!"

HAZCUSEAC

#5 "I don't know this man you're talking about!"

PONSTEEMRI

#6 "Eight months' wages would not buy enough bread for each one to have a bite!"

LIHPIP

WHO SAID THAT? JUMBLE

Using the quotes below as clues, try to unscramble the mixed-up letters to form the names of the books of the Bible where the quotes are found.

#1 "Ever since the world was created, people have seen the earth and sky. Through everything God made, they can clearly see his invisible qualities—his eternal power and divine nature. So they have no excuse for not knowing God."

NOSARM

#2 "The LORD did not set his heart on you and choose you because you were more numerous than other nations, for you were the smallest of all nations!"

YEMOURETOND

#3 "As a face is reflected in water, so the heart reflects the real person."

VORSPERB

#4 "The one sitting on the throne said, 'Look, I am making everything new!' And then he said to me, 'Write this down, for what I tell you is trustworthy and true.'"

TEENILVARO

#5 "Take control of what I say, O LORD, and guard my lips."

MASSLP

#6 "Resist the devil, and he will flee from you."

EMJAS

WHO SAID THAT? JUMBLE

Using the quotes below as clues, try to unscramble the mixed-up letters to form the names of the books of the Bible where the quotes are found.

#1 "Look at what was happening to you before you began to lay the foundation of the LORD's Temple."

GIGAHA

#2 "However, the money that was contributed for guilt offerings and sin offerings was not brought into the LORD's Temple. It was given to the priests for their own use."

SOCKSDENING

#3 "Using acacia wood, construct a square altar. . . . Make horns for each of its four corners so that the horns and altar are all one piece."

SEDUXO

#4 "Let us hold tightly without wavering to the hope we affirm, for God can be trusted to keep his promise."

SHEWBER

#5 "God blesses those who hunger and thirst for justice, for they will be satisfied."

WAHTMET

#6 "Arise, O LORD, and let your enemies be scattered! Let them flee before you!"

BRUNMES

106

WHO SAID THAT? JUMBLE

Using the quotes below as clues, try to unscramble the mixed-up letters to form the names of the books of the Bible where the quotes are found.

#1 "The Holy Spirit produces this kind of fruit in our lives: love, joy, peace, patience, kindness, goodness, faithfulness, gentleness, and self-control."

ASLANGAIT

#2 "All Scripture is inspired by God and is useful to teach us what is true and to make us realize what is wrong in our lives. It corrects us when we are wrong and teaches us to do what is right."

DOONYCHETTSMI

#3 "I am the spring crocus blooming on the Sharon Plain, the lily of the valley."

NONSFOGGOSS

#4 "The LORD gives his own reward for doing good and for being loyal, and I refused to kill you even when the LORD placed you in my power, for you are the LORD's anointed one."

STIRULSMEAF

#5 "God saw that the earth had become corrupt and was filled with violence."

ISGEENS

#6 "I planted the seed in your hearts, and Apollos watered it, but it was God who made it grow."

TINORFICASSNIRTH

WHO SAID THAT? JUMBLE

Using the quotes below as clues, try to unscramble the mixed-up letters to form the names of the people responsible for the quotes.

#1 "Why are you interfering with me, Jesus, Son of the Most High God? In the name of God, I beg you, don't torture me!"

GENIOL

#2 "Lord, doesn't it seem unfair to you that my sister just sits here while I do all the work? Tell her to come and help me."

RAMAHT

#3 "You must be the only person in Jerusalem who hasn't heard about all the things that have happened there the last few days."

PASOLEC

#4 "Please, sir, give me this water! Then I'll never be thirsty again, and I won't have to come here to get water."

NANTOWAIRMAMAS

#5 "You don't know what you're talking about! You don't realize that it's better for you that one man should die for the people than for the whole nation to be destroyed."

ASCHAPAI

#6 "Though his ministry follows mine, I'm not even worthy to be his slave and untie the straps of his sandal."

THISBANJOHPETT

WHO SAID THAT? JUMBLE

Using the quotes below as clues, try to unscramble the mixed-up letters to form the names of the people responsible for the quotes.

#1 "Give me an understanding heart so that I can govern your people well and know the difference between right and wrong. For who by himself is able to govern this great people of yours?"

MOONLOS

#2 "Please let me inherit a double share of your spirit."

SELHAI

#3 "Why haven't you repaired the Temple? Don't use any more money for your own needs. From now on, it must all be spent on Temple repairs."

HISJOKANG

#4 "Live in the land and serve the king of Babylon, and all will go well for you."

ALADEIGH

#5 "O LORD, God of our ancestors, you alone are the God who is in heaven. You are ruler of all the kingdoms of the earth. You are powerful and mighty; no one can stand against you!"

TAJOHASHPEH

#6 "Let us rebuild the wall of Jerusalem and end this disgrace!"

MHEENAIH

WHO SAID THAT? JUMBLE

Using the quotes below as clues, try to unscramble the mixed-up letters to form the names of the people responsible for the quotes.

#1 "You should not have rejoiced when the people of Judah suffered such misfortune. You should not have spoken arrogantly in that terrible time of trouble."

H	O	D	I	B	A	A

#2 "Come, let us return to the LORD. He has torn us to pieces; now he will heal us. He has injured us; now he will bandage our wounds."

A	E	S	H	O

#3 "O LORD, protect your people with your shepherd's staff; lead your flock, your special possession. Though they live alone in a thicket on the heights of Mount Carmel, let them graze in the fertile pastures of Bashan and Gilead as they did long ago."

I	M	H	A	C

#4 "Didn't I say before I left home that you would do this, LORD? That is why I ran away to Tarshish! I knew that you are a merciful and compassionate God, slow to get angry and filled with unfailing love. You are eager to turn back from destroying people."

N	A	J	H	O

#5 "As the waters fill the sea, the earth will be filled with an awareness of the glory of the LORD."

A	K	K	U	B	K	A	H

#6 "Guard your heart; remain loyal to the wife of your youth."

C	H	I	L	A	M	A

WHO SAID THAT? JUMBLE

Using the quotes below as clues, try to unscramble the mixed-up letters to form the names of the people responsible for the quotes.

#1 "Understand this, my dear brothers and sisters: You must all be quick to listen, slow to speak, and slow to get angry."

M	E	S	A	J

#2 "You have provided a long period of peace for us Jews and with foresight have enacted reforms for us."

S	U	L	L	R	E	T	T	U

#3 "I sent for you at once, and it was good of you to come. Now we are all here, waiting before God to hear the message the LORD has given you."

N	I	R	C	O	U	S	E	L

#4 "Look, I see the heavens opened and the Son of Man standing in the place of honor at God's right hand!"

P	E	H	N	T	E	S

#5 "Men of Israel, take care what you are planning to do to these men!"

L	E	G	A	L	I	M	A

#6 "Let me have this power, too, so that when I lay my hands on people, they will receive the Holy Spirit!"

T	O	O	R	S	I	R	R	N	E	C	H	E	E	M	S

WHO SAID THAT? JUMBLE

Using the quotes below as clues, try to unscramble the mixed-up letters to form the names of the people responsible for the quotes.

#1 "Brother Saul, the Lord Jesus, who appeared to you on the road, has sent me so that you might regain your sight and be filled with the Holy Spirit."

N	A	A	N	S	I	A

#2 "If you agree that I am a true believer in the Lord, come and stay at my home."

D	A	I	L	Y

#3 "Listen, you Jews, if this were a case involving some wrongdoing or a serious crime, I would have a reason to accept your case."

L	I	L	O	G	A

#4 "Are you willing to go to Jerusalem and stand trial before me there?"

T	U	F	S	E	S

#5 "He could have been set free if he hadn't appealed to Caesar."

P	A	P	A	R	I	G

#6 "When you sit on your glorious throne, we want to sit in places of honor next to you, one on your right and the other on your left."

M	A	J	J	A	H	O	D	E	N	N	S

WHO SAID THAT? JUMBLE

Using the quotes below as clues, try to unscramble the mixed-up letters to form the names of the people responsible for the quotes.

#1 "Draw your sword and kill me, so that they can't say, 'A woman killed him.'"

C	A	H	B	I	M	E	E	L	

#2 "If you give me victory over the Ammonites, I will give to the LORD whatever comes out of my house to meet me when I return in triumph. I will sacrifice it as a burnt offering."

H	E	J	H	P	A	T	H	

#3 "LORD, please let the man of God come back to us again and give us more instructions about this son who is to be born."

A	H	O	M	N	A	

#4 "You've been making fun of me and telling me lies! Now please tell me how you can be tied up securely."

L	A	D	E	H	I	L	

#5 "May the LORD bless you with the security of another marriage."

I	M	O	N	A	

#6 "My heart rejoices in the LORD! The LORD has made me strong. Now I have an answer for my enemies; I rejoice because you rescued me."

A	N	H	A	H	N	

113

WHO SAID THAT? JUMBLE

Using the quotes below as clues, try to unscramble the mixed-up letters to form the names of the people responsible for the quotes.

#1 "Speak, your servant is listening."

E	M	A	L	U	S	

#2 "The LORD has forgiven you, and you won't die for this sin. Nevertheless, because you have shown utter contempt for the LORD by doing this, your child will die."

H	A	T	N	A	N	

#3 "What's the trouble? Why should the son of a king look so dejected morning after morning?"

A	D	B	A	N	J	O	

#4 "I am in love with Tamar, my brother Absalom's sister."

N	A	M	N	O	

#5 "I wanted you to ask the king why he brought me back from Geshur if he didn't intend to see me. I might as well have stayed there. Let me see the king; if he finds me guilty of anything, then let him kill me."

M	O	L	S	A	A	B	

#6 "Let me choose 12,000 men to start out after David tonight. I will catch up with him while he is weary and discouraged. He and his troops will panic, and everyone will run away. Then I will kill only the king."

H	O	T	E	L	H	A	P	I	H	

WHO SAID THAT? JUMBLE

Using the quotes below as clues, try to unscramble the mixed-up letters to form the names of the people responsible for the quotes.

#1 "Let me return to my own country."

D	A	A	H	D

#2 "Take ten of these pieces, for this is what the LORD, the God of Israel, says: 'I am about to tear the kingdom from the hand of Solomon.'"

J	A	H	A	I	H

#3 "What is your advice? How should I answer these people who want me to lighten the burdens imposed by my father?"

B	O	O	R	H	E	M	A

#4 "Disguise yourself so that no one will recognize you as my wife. Then go to the prophet Ahijah at Shiloh—the man who told me I would become king."

O	M	A	J	O	R	E	B

#5 "How much longer will you waver, hobbling between two opinions? If the LORD is God, follow him! But if Baal is God, then follow him!"

J	I	L	H	A	E

#6 "Are you the king of Israel or not? Get up and eat something, and don't worry about it. I'll get you Naboth's vineyard!"

B	E	E	L	Z	E	J

WHO SAID THAT? JUMBLE

Using the quotes below as clues, try to unscramble the mixed-up letters to form the names of the people responsible for the quotes.

#1 "If you keep quiet at a time like this, deliverance and relief for the Jews will arise from some other place, but you and your relatives will die. Who knows if perhaps you were made queen for just such a time as this?"

CIRDAMEO

#2 "If I have found favor with the king, and if it pleases the king to grant my request, I ask that my life and the lives of my people will be spared."

EQUESTRENEH

#3 "What is your request? I will give it to you, even if it is half the kingdom!"

KNIXREXGES

#4 "Whom would the king wish to honor more than me?"

MAANH

#5 "I will sing of the LORD's unfailing love forever! Young and old will hear of your faithfulness."

NEHTA

#6 "God will provide a sheep for the burnt offering, my son."

MABARAH

WHO SAID THAT? JUMBLE

Using the quotes below as clues, try to unscramble the mixed-up letters to form the names of the books of the Bible where the quotes are found.

#1 "LORD, may all your enemies die like Sisera! But may those who love you rise like the sun in all its power!"

JEDSUG

#2 "You must have the same attitude that Christ Jesus had."

PINISHLAPPI

#3 "That's the whole story. Here now is my final conclusion: Fear God and obey his commands, for this is everyone's duty."

SATISLECCESE

#4 "Now you have been united with Christ Jesus. Once you were far away from God, but now you have been brought near to him through the blood of Christ."

ENISHAPES

#5 "Remind the believers to submit to the government and its officers. They should be obedient, always ready to do what is good."

SITTU

#6 "The faithful love of the LORD never ends! His mercies never cease."

TELOSMANTIAN

WHO SAID THAT? JUMBLE

Using the quotes below as clues, try to unscramble the mixed-up letters to form the names of the people responsible for the quotes.

#1 "I accept all blame in this matter, my lord. Please listen to what I have to say. I know Nabal is a wicked and ill-tempered man; please don't pay any attention to him. He is a fool, just as his name suggests."

BIALIGA

#2 "God Almighty appeared to me at Luz in the land of Canaan and blessed me."

AJBOC

#3 "'O Sovereign LORD,' I said, 'I can't speak for you! I'm too young!'"

HEEMAJIR

#4 "You brought this man to me, accusing him of leading a revolt. I have examined him thoroughly on this point in your presence and find him innocent."

TENIPOPALISTU

#5 "I bring you good news that will bring great joy to all people. The Savior—yes, the Messiah, the Lord—has been born today in Bethlehem, the city of David!"

FLODOLEHGARTEN

#6 "Sovereign Lord, now let your servant die in peace, as you have promised. I have seen your salvation."

MONIES

WHO SAID THAT? JUMBLE

Using the quotes below as clues, try to unscramble the mixed-up letters to form the names of the people responsible for the quotes.

#1 "My little daughter is dying. Please come and lay your hands on her; heal her so she can live."

S A R U J I

#2 "Jesus, Son of David, have mercy on me! . . . My rabbi, I want to see!"

A I S T R A M B U E

#3 "You will know which one to arrest when I greet him with a kiss."

D O C T A I R J A U S S I

#4 "Hail! King of the Jews!"

D O S S L E I R

#5 "This is all your fault! I put my servant into your arms, but now that she's pregnant she treats me with contempt. The LORD will show who's wrong—you or me!"

I S A A R

#6 "I have struggled hard with my sister, and I'm winning!"

H E R L A C

WHO SAID THAT? JUMBLE

Using the quotes below as clues, try to unscramble the mixed-up letters to form the names of the people responsible for the quotes.

#1 "Please be kind to me, and let me marry her. I will give you whatever you ask. No matter what dowry or gift you demand, I will gladly pay it—just give me the girl as my wife."

> MCHEESH

#2 "Do you know where they are pasturing their sheep?"

> SOPJEH

#3 "I saw a grapevine in front of me. The vine had three branches that began to bud and blossom, and soon it produced clusters of ripe grapes."

> RUBRACEEP

#4 "You're just lazy! Lazy! That's why you're saying, 'Let us go and offer sacrifices to the LORD.'"

> HAPOHAR

#5 "With the jawbone of a donkey, I've piled them in heaps! With the jawbone of a donkey, I've killed a thousand men!"

> MOSSAN

#6 "My father has made trouble for us all! A command like that only hurts us. See how refreshed I am now that I have eaten this little bit of honey."

> NOTAJNAH

120

WHO SAID THAT? JUMBLE

Using the quotes below as clues, try to unscramble the mixed-up letters to form the names of the people responsible for the quotes.

#1 "Doesn't your reverence for God give you confidence? Doesn't your life of integrity give you hope?"

IZALPEH

#2 "Help us, O God of our salvation! Help us for the glory of your name. Save us and forgive our sins for the honor of your name."

PAASH

#3 "Listen! It's the voice of someone shouting, 'Clear the way through the wilderness for the LORD! Make a straight highway through the wasteland for our God!'"

AHIASI

#4 "Son of man, pretend you are being sent into exile. Pack the few items an exile could carry, and leave your home to go somewhere else. Do this right in front of the people so they can see you. For perhaps they will pay attention to this, even though they are such rebels."

KLIEZEE

#5 "How great are his signs, how powerful his wonders! His kingdom will last forever, his rule through all generations."

ZANZARBECHUNDE

#6 "My God sent his angel to shut the lions' mouths so that they would not hurt me, for I have been found innocent in his sight. And I have not wronged you, Your Majesty."

NEALID

WHO SAID THAT? JUMBLE

Using the quotes below as clues, try to unscramble the mixed-up letters to form the names of the people responsible for the quotes.

#1 "Stand in silence in the presence of the Sovereign LORD, for the awesome day of the LORD's judgment is near. The LORD has prepared his people for a great slaughter and has chosen their executioners."

HIAPAZHEN

#2 "I looked up and saw four animal horns. 'What are these?' I asked the angel who was talking with me."

CRAZIHEHA

#3 "Are we not all children of the same Father? Are we not all created by the same God? Then why do we betray each other, violating the covenant of our ancestors?"

LAMACIH

#4 "Go to Bethlehem and search carefully for the child. And when you find him, come back and tell me so that I can go and worship him, too!"

GHONERKID

#5 "If you are the Son of God, tell these stones to become loaves of bread."

VEEDLITH

#6 "Lord, I am not worthy to have you come into my home. Just say the word from where you are, and my servant will be healed."

ORETUCINN

WHO SAID THAT? JUMBLE

Using the quotes below as clues, try to unscramble the mixed-up letters to form the names of the people responsible for the quotes.

#1 "I am far too old to go with the king to Jerusalem."

ILZRABALI

#2 "Give him all of it. I am content just to have you safely back again, my lord the king!"

PISHHETOMBEH

#3 "May my lord King David live forever!"

SABBETHAH

#4 "May the LORD, the God of my lord the king, decree that it happen. And may the LORD be with Solomon as he has been with you, my lord the king, and may he make Solomon's reign even greater than yours!"

ABNEAHI

#5 "Praise the LORD today for giving David a wise son to be king of the great nation of Israel."

IMAHR

#6 "Everything I heard in my country about your achievements and wisdom is true! I didn't believe what was said until I arrived here and saw it with my own eyes. In fact, I had not heard the half of it! Your wisdom and prosperity are far beyond what I was told."

FESEQUONEHAB

WHO SAID THAT? JUMBLE

Using the quotes below as clues, try to unscramble the mixed-up letters to form the names of the people responsible for the quotes.

#1 "In a vision I saw all Israel scattered on the mountains, like sheep without a shepherd."

I	M	A	I	C	H	A

#2 "I thought he would certainly come out to meet me! I expected him to wave his hand over the leprosy and call on the name of the LORD his God and heal me!"

M	A	N	A	N	A

#3 "How could a nobody like me ever accomplish such great things?"

Z	A	A	L	E	H

#4 "Take her to the soldiers in front of the Temple, and kill anyone who tries to rescue her. She must not be killed in the Temple of the LORD."

A	D	O	H	E	J	A	I

#5 "Please speak to us in Aramaic, for we understand it well. Don't speak in Hebrew, for the people on the wall will hear."

I	M	A	K	I	L	E

#6 "Bend down, O LORD, and listen! Open your eyes, O LORD, and see! Listen to Sennacherib's words of defiance against the living God."

Z	E	E	H	K	A	I	H

WHO SAID THAT? JUMBLE

Using the quotes below as clues, try to unscramble the mixed-up letters to form the names of the books of the Bible where the quotes are found.

#1 "Though I am far away from you, my heart is with you. And I rejoice that you are living as you should and that your faith in Christ is strong."

S N A S L O C I O S

#2 "The warriors released the prisoners and handed over the plunder in the sight of the leaders and all the people."

C L O S S O I N D R E N C H E C

#3 "This is a permanent law for you, to purify the people of Israel from their sins, making them right with the LORD once each year."

V E T S U L I C I

#4 "Dear friend, don't let this bad example influence you. Follow only what is good. Remember that those who do good prove that they are God's children, and those who do evil prove that they do not know God."

D O H T R I N J H

#5 "Amasa convinced all the men of Judah, and they responded unanimously. They sent word to the king, 'Return to us, and bring back all who are with you.'"

C U L D O N S A M E E S

#6 "I always thank my God when I pray for you."

H O M P N E I L

BOX OF CLUES JUMBLE

Unscramble the Jumbles, one letter to each square, to form ordinary words. Then arrange circled letters to solve the Mystery Answer, below.

#1 VEE

#2 MAAD

#3 SARGS

#4 LETTCA

#5 DARFOBE

#6 SEERBATH

#7 MIMFENTAR

#8 DILIPUMELT

BOX OF CLUES

STUMPED? MAYBE YOU CAN FIND A CLUE BELOW. (CLUES ARE NOT IN ORDER.)

first woman
outlawed
respires
beef or dairy
some blades
first man
heavens
increased

MYSTERY ANSWER:

BOX OF CLUES JUMBLE

Unscramble the Jumbles, one letter to each square, to form ordinary words. Then arrange circled letters to solve the Mystery Answer, below.

#1   E W J

#2   I N V E

#3   F I C H E

#4   R A V O S I

#5   V A O J H E H

#6   T A C O V E D A

#7   L O O N R U C E S

#8   M E E R D O T N I P

BOX OF CLUES

STUMPED? MAYBE YOU CAN FIND A CLUE BELOW. (CLUES ARE NOT IN ORDER.)

God
one who brings salvation
supporter
head of the tribe
Israelite
advisor
fruitful branch
rescue

MYSTERY ANSWER:

127

BOX OF CLUES JUMBLE

Unscramble the Jumbles, one letter to each square, to form ordinary words. Then arrange circled letters to solve the Mystery Answer, below.

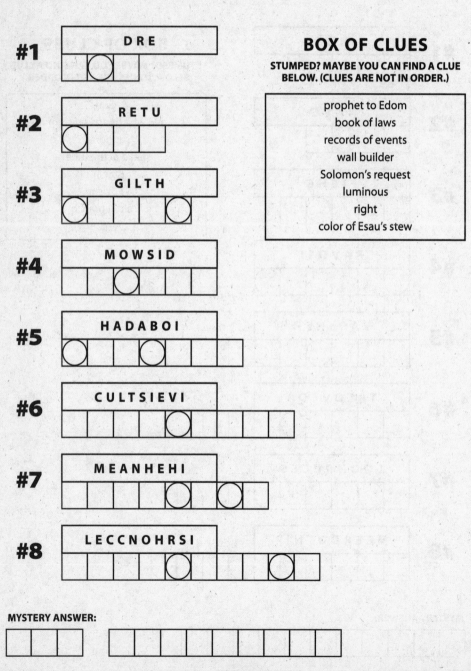

#1 DRE

#2 RETU

#3 GILTH

#4 MOWSID

#5 HADABOI

#6 CULTSIEVI

#7 MEANHEHI

#8 LECCNOHRSI

BOX OF CLUES

STUMPED? MAYBE YOU CAN FIND A CLUE BELOW. (CLUES ARE NOT IN ORDER.)

prophet to Edom
book of laws
records of events
wall builder
Solomon's request
luminous
right
color of Esau's stew

MYSTERY ANSWER:

128

BOX OF CLUES JUMBLE

Unscramble the Jumbles, one letter to each square, to form ordinary words. Then arrange circled letters to solve the Mystery Answer, below.

#1 NSO

#2 ROPO

#3 DRUOP

#4 CREPNI

#5 TEFRCEP

#6 TUROVISU

#7 YOCHIPERT

#8 REEBARLATE

BOX OF CLUES

STUMPED? MAYBE YOU CAN FIND A CLUE BELOW. (CLUES ARE NOT IN ORDER.)

flawless
of good moral standing
storyteller
full of arrogance
one with two faces
indigent
male offspring
royal son

MYSTERY ANSWER:

☐☐☐☐☐☐☐ **OF** ☐☐☐☐☐☐☐☐☐

BOX OF CLUES JUMBLE

Unscramble the Jumbles, one letter to each square, to form ordinary words. Then arrange circled letters to solve the Mystery Answer, below.

#1 P C U

#2 D E H A

#3 S H U O E

#4 S U P E R U

#5 S I M E E N E

#6 S O M D E W A

#7 N E D S O O G S

#8 V O W S E R L O F

BOX OF CLUES

STUMPED? MAYBE YOU CAN FIND A CLUE BELOW. (CLUES ARE NOT IN ORDER.)

abode
drinking vessel
foes
track
decency
brims
neck attachment
pastures

MYSTERY ANSWER:

BOX OF CLUES JUMBLE

Unscramble the Jumbles, one letter to each square, to form ordinary words. Then arrange circled letters to solve the Mystery Answer, below.

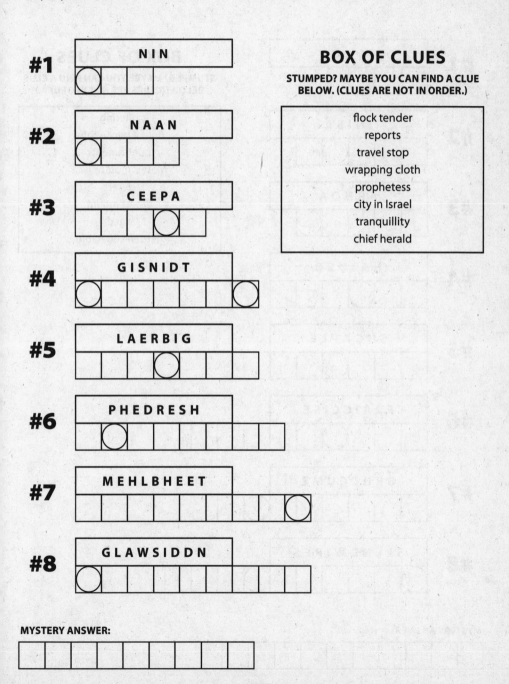

#1 N I N

#2 N A A N

#3 C E E P A

#4 G I S N I D T

#5 L A E R B I G

#6 P H E D R E S H

#7 M E H L B H E E T

#8 G L A W S I D D N

BOX OF CLUES

STUMPED? MAYBE YOU CAN FIND A CLUE BELOW. (CLUES ARE NOT IN ORDER.)

flock tender
reports
travel stop
wrapping cloth
prophetess
city in Israel
tranquillity
chief herald

MYSTERY ANSWER:

BOX OF CLUES JUMBLE

Unscramble the Jumbles, one letter to each square, to form ordinary words. Then arrange circled letters to solve the Mystery Answer, below.

#1 DLO

#2 INISA

#3 ARNOA

#4 HAJUSO

#5 SUGAPLE

#6 FRAICCISE

#7 BRUCCUME

#8 SLENDWIRES

BOX OF CLUES

STUMPED? MAYBE YOU CAN FIND A CLUE BELOW. (CLUES ARE NOT IN ORDER.)

offering
one of two faithful
punishments
Moses' mouthpiece
desert
desert mount
aged
garden vegetable

MYSTERY ANSWER:

BOX OF CLUES JUMBLE

Unscramble the Jumbles, one letter to each square, to form ordinary words. Then arrange circled letters to solve the Mystery Answer, below.

#1 RAK

#2 LULSB

#3 LEEPOP

#4 DEERME

#5 WARBINO

#6 SHEABILTS

#7 TENNOCAV

#8 REINETONGA

BOX OF CLUES

STUMPED? MAYBE YOU CAN FIND A CLUE BELOW. (CLUES ARE NOT IN ORDER.)

unbreakable agreement
inhabitants
large water vessel
create
family line
sacrificial animals
chromatic arc
buy back

MYSTERY ANSWER:

BOX OF CLUES JUMBLE

Unscramble the Jumbles, one letter to each square, to form ordinary words. Then arrange circled letters to solve the Mystery Answer, below.

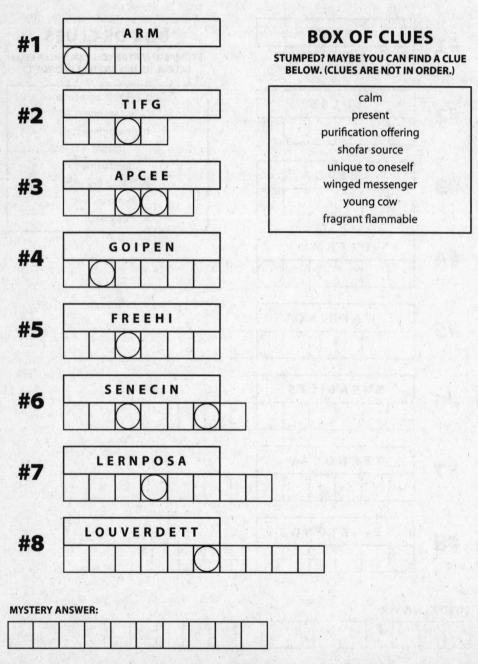

#1 A R M

#2 T I F G

#3 A P C E E

#4 G O I P E N

#5 F R E E H I

#6 S E N E C I N

#7 L E R N P O S A

#8 L O U V E R D E T T

BOX OF CLUES
STUMPED? MAYBE YOU CAN FIND A CLUE BELOW. (CLUES ARE NOT IN ORDER.)

calm
present
purification offering
shofar source
unique to oneself
winged messenger
young cow
fragrant flammable

MYSTERY ANSWER:

BOX OF CLUES JUMBLE

Unscramble the Jumbles, one letter to each square, to form ordinary words. Then arrange circled letters to solve the Mystery Answer, below.

#1 Y R C

#2 N U F O D

#3 D O C K M E

#4 P H I P D E W

#5 G R I V A N E

#6 L O A G T O G H

#7 H O X H U R T I S

#8 N E S H A G M E E T

BOX OF CLUES

STUMPED? MAYBE YOU CAN FIND A CLUE BELOW. (CLUES ARE NOT IN ORDER.)

killing hill
discovered
bitter drink
lashed
prayer garden
scorned
noon
wail

MYSTERY ANSWER:

BOX OF CLUES JUMBLE

Unscramble the Jumbles, one letter to each square, to form ordinary words. Then arrange circled letters to solve the Mystery Answer, below.

#1 E S E

#2 P Y A R

#3 A L O C K

#4 N Y K O D E

#5 N A A N S H O

#6 S C R E B N A H

#7 J A S M U R E E L

#8 D U T T E R S N I C

BOX OF CLUES

STUMPED? MAYBE YOU CAN FIND A CLUE BELOW. (CLUES ARE NOT IN ORDER.)

directed
beast of burden
city in Israel
look
limbs
cry of exaltation
outer garment
talk to God

MYSTERY ANSWER:

BOX OF CLUES JUMBLE

Unscramble the Jumbles, one letter to each square, to form ordinary words. Then arrange circled letters to solve the Mystery Answer, below.

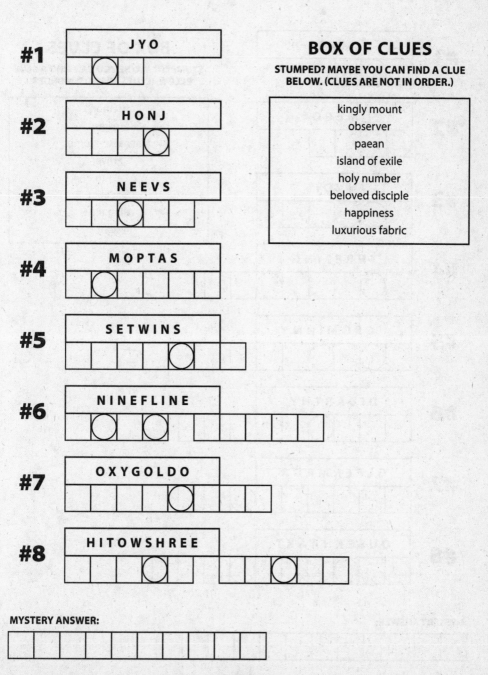

#1 JYO

#2 HONJ

#3 NEEVS

#4 MOPTAS

#5 SETWINS

#6 NINEFLINE

#7 OXYGOLDO

#8 HITOWSHREE

BOX OF CLUES

STUMPED? MAYBE YOU CAN FIND A CLUE BELOW. (CLUES ARE NOT IN ORDER.)

kingly mount
observer
paean
island of exile
holy number
beloved disciple
happiness
luxurious fabric

MYSTERY ANSWER:

BOX OF CLUES JUMBLE

Unscramble the Jumbles, one letter to each square, to form ordinary words. Then arrange circled letters to solve the Mystery Answer, below.

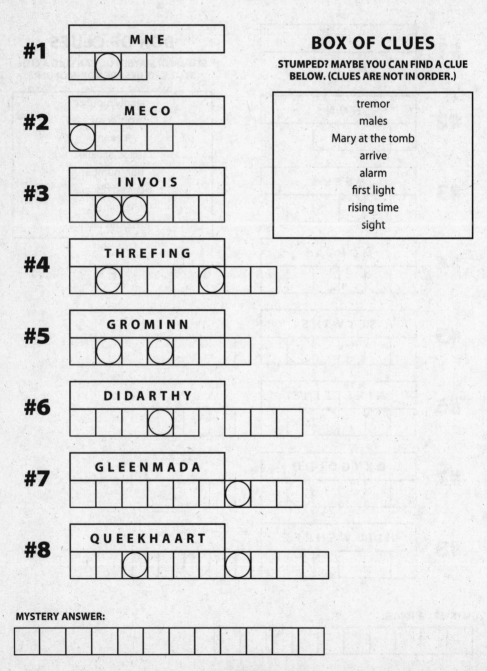

#1 MNE

#2 MECO

#3 INVOIS

#4 THREFING

#5 GROMINN

#6 DIDARTHY

#7 GLEENMADA

#8 QUEEKHAART

BOX OF CLUES

STUMPED? MAYBE YOU CAN FIND A CLUE BELOW. (CLUES ARE NOT IN ORDER.)

tremor
males
Mary at the tomb
arrive
alarm
first light
rising time
sight

MYSTERY ANSWER:

BOX OF CLUES JUMBLE

Unscramble the Jumbles, one letter to each square, to form ordinary words. Then arrange circled letters to solve the Mystery Answer, below.

#1 VELO

#2 HITFA

#3 TUPIRY

#4 LIMIHYUT

#5 ENEDIBECO

#6 VERCENREE

#7 SNELGESTEN

#8 RONSOFTCELL

BOX OF CLUES

STUMPED? MAYBE YOU CAN FIND A CLUE BELOW. (CLUES ARE NOT IN ORDER.)

belief without sight

mild manner

modesty

adoration

restraint

conformity

innocence

respect

MYSTERY ANSWER:

BOX OF CLUES JUMBLE

Unscramble the Jumbles, one letter to each square, to form ordinary words. Then arrange circled letters to solve the Mystery Answer, below.

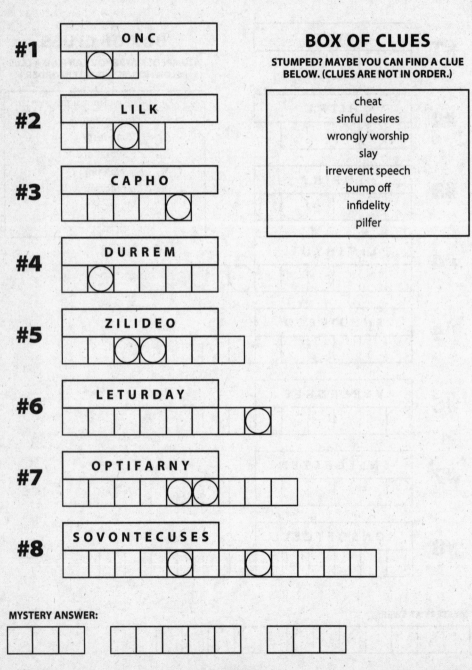

#1 O N C

#2 L I L K

#3 C A P H O

#4 D U R R E M

#5 Z I L I D E O

#6 L E T U R D A Y

#7 O P T I F A R N Y

#8 S O V O N T E C U S E S

BOX OF CLUES

STUMPED? MAYBE YOU CAN FIND A CLUE
BELOW. (CLUES ARE NOT IN ORDER.)

cheat
sinful desires
wrongly worship
slay
irreverent speech
bump off
infidelity
pilfer

MYSTERY ANSWER:

BOX OF CLUES JUMBLE

Unscramble the Jumbles, one letter to each square, to form ordinary words. Then arrange circled letters to solve the Mystery Answer, below.

#1 W Y A

#2 S W I E

#3 R O G L Y

#4 I T R U V E

#5 S L E D B E S

#6 D J E M T U N G

#7 G O L D N W E E K

#8 S N E M G R E E S S

BOX OF CLUES

STUMPED? MAYBE YOU CAN FIND A CLUE BELOW. (CLUES ARE NOT IN ORDER.)

prudence
angels
astute
grandeur
learning
consecrated
path
positive quality

MYSTERY ANSWER:

☐☐☐☐☐ **O F** ☐☐☐☐☐

BOX OF CLUES JUMBLE

Unscramble the Jumbles, one letter to each square, to form ordinary words. Then arrange circled letters to solve the Mystery Answer, below.

#1 BOJ

#2 UALP

#3 SOMES

#4 THIRSC

#5 HARAMBA

#6 NAJAHNOT

#7 HIREZAACH

#8 HUMSHTEALE

BOX OF CLUES

STUMPED? MAYBE YOU CAN FIND A CLUE BELOW. (CLUES ARE NOT IN ORDER.)

church planter
promised one
afflicted friend
ancient ancient
father of nations
faithful friend
mountain man
myrtle tree prophet

MYSTERY ANSWER:

BOX OF CLUES JUMBLE

Unscramble the Jumbles, one letter to each square, to form ordinary words. Then arrange circled letters to solve the Mystery Answer, below.

#1 ERD

#2 YITC

#3 ZHROA

#4 LEGDIA

#5 DOGIDEM

#6 THERANZA

#7 CASSAMUD

#8 POPACADIAC

BOX OF CLUES

STUMPED? MAYBE YOU CAN FIND A CLUE BELOW. (CLUES ARE NOT IN ORDER.)

small town in Galilee
King Jabin's town
metropolis
balmy hill country
valley of mourning
provincial outpost
Aramean capital
split sea

MYSTERY ANSWER:

BOX OF CLUES JUMBLE

Unscramble the Jumbles, one letter to each square, to form ordinary words. Then arrange circled letters to solve the Mystery Answer, below.

#1 USAE

#2 NESOT

#3 LEHBET

#4 MOPERIS

#5 ROYJUNE

#6 VERPOIDD

#7 WARISTAY

#8 CADDETENNS

BOX OF CLUES

STUMPED? MAYBE YOU CAN FIND A CLUE BELOW. (CLUES ARE NOT IN ORDER.)

up and down flight
tricked twin
travel
vow
supplied
wilderness pillow
progeny
"house of God"

MYSTERY ANSWER:

BOX OF CLUES JUMBLE

Unscramble the Jumbles, one letter to each square, to form ordinary words. Then arrange circled letters to solve the Mystery Answer, below.

#1 N S I

#2 B S F I

#3 V E C T O

#4 D R U M E R

#5 N U T T L O G Y

#6 S E E J O L A I S U

#7 M Y L S H E P A B

#8 B Y R D A C E E U H

BOX OF CLUES

STUMPED? MAYBE YOU CAN FIND A CLUE BELOW. (CLUES ARE NOT IN ORDER.)

irreverence
overeater
tales
dispatch
crave
excessive indulgence
petty concerns
transgression

MYSTERY ANSWER:

145

BOX OF CLUES JUMBLE

Unscramble the Jumbles, one letter to each square, to form ordinary words. Then arrange circled letters to solve the Mystery Answer, below.

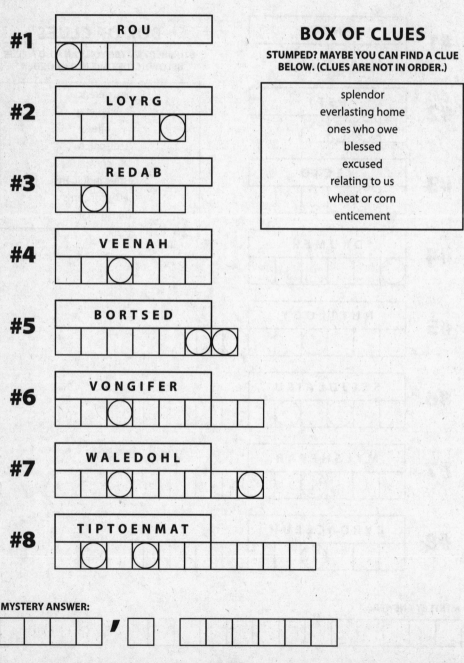

#1 ROU

#2 LOYRG

#3 REDAB

#4 VEENAH

#5 BORTSED

#6 VONGIFER

#7 WALEDOHL

#8 TIPTOENMAT

BOX OF CLUES

STUMPED? MAYBE YOU CAN FIND A CLUE BELOW. (CLUES ARE NOT IN ORDER.)

splendor
everlasting home
ones who owe
blessed
excused
relating to us
wheat or corn
enticement

MYSTERY ANSWER:

146

BOX OF CLUES JUMBLE

Unscramble the Jumbles, one letter to each square, to form ordinary words. Then arrange circled letters to solve the Mystery Answer, below.

#1 SAA

#2 HUJE

#3 NOBDA

#4 DOGINE

#5 MARGASH

#6 KEEZHIAH

#7 JIMOKAEHI

#8 LAZERZBASH

BOX OF CLUES

STUMPED? MAYBE YOU CAN FIND A CLUE BELOW. (CLUES ARE NOT IN ORDER.)

son of Abijam
son of Ahaz
son of Jehoshaphat
son of Joash
son of Anath
son of Hillel
son of Josiah
son of Nebuchadnezzar

MYSTERY ANSWER:

☐☐☐☐☐☐ **AND** ☐☐☐☐☐

BOX OF CLUES JUMBLE

Unscramble the Jumbles, one letter to each square, to form ordinary words. Then arrange circled letters to solve the Mystery Answer, below.

#1 GEA

#2 LEPH

#3 GAIME

#4 WRENSA

#5 NEFRUCA

#6 NOTNNICE

#7 ROOPREVEW

#8 IDUKSAGRIN

BOX OF CLUES

STUMPED? MAYBE YOU CAN FIND A CLUE BELOW. (CLUES ARE NOT IN ORDER.)

vanquish

aid

reflection

hot spot

number of years

without fault

Persian ruler

response

MYSTERY ANSWER:

BOX OF CLUES JUMBLE

Unscramble the Jumbles, one letter to each square, to form ordinary words. Then arrange circled letters to solve the Mystery Answer, below.

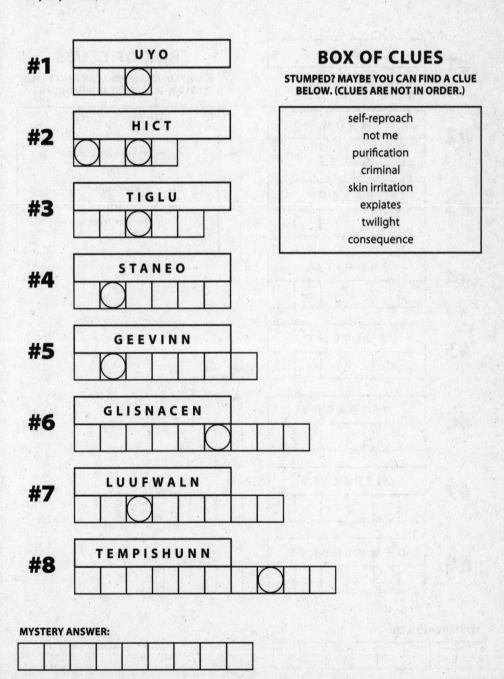

#1 U Y O

#2 H I C T

#3 T I G L U

#4 S T A N E O

#5 G E E V I N N

#6 G L I S N A C E N

#7 L U U F W A L N

#8 T E M P I S H U N N

BOX OF CLUES

STUMPED? MAYBE YOU CAN FIND A CLUE BELOW. (CLUES ARE NOT IN ORDER.)

self-reproach
not me
purification
criminal
skin irritation
expiates
twilight
consequence

MYSTERY ANSWER:

BOX OF CLUES JUMBLE

Unscramble the Jumbles, one letter to each square, to form ordinary words. Then arrange circled letters to solve the Mystery Answer, below.

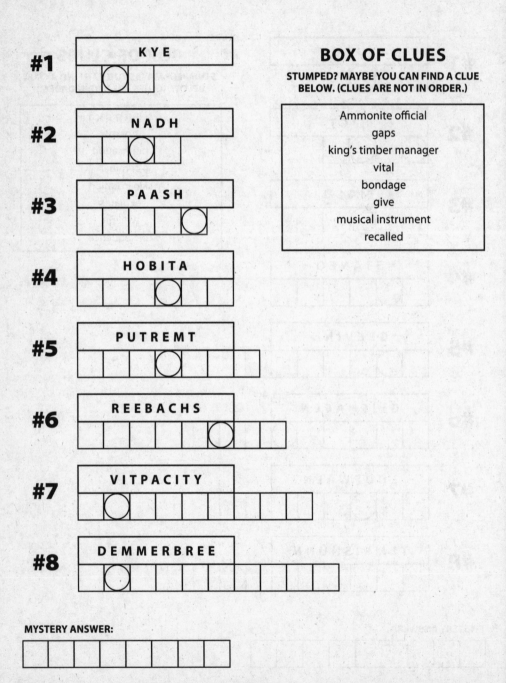

#1 KYE

#2 NADH

#3 PAASH

#4 HOBITA

#5 PUTREMT

#6 REEBACHS

#7 VITPACITY

#8 DEMMERBREE

BOX OF CLUES

STUMPED? MAYBE YOU CAN FIND A CLUE BELOW. (CLUES ARE NOT IN ORDER.)

Ammonite official
gaps
king's timber manager
vital
bondage
give
musical instrument
recalled

MYSTERY ANSWER:

TRIVIA JUMBLE

Unscramble the Jumbles, one letter to each square, to form words suggested by the trivia clues.

#1 SEJAM

CLUE: Book written by the leader of the Jerusalem council

#2 WHAMTET

CLUE: Book written by a tax collector

#3 BESHWER

CLUE: Book written for Jewish converts

#4 MOTTHYI

CLUE: Book written to a missionary friend

#5 NINSHOCARIT

CLUE: Book with a love chapter

Arrange the circled letters to solve the Mystery Answer.

What is the name of writings that followed Christ's birth?

MYSTERY ANSWER:

TRIVIA JUMBLE

Unscramble the Jumbles, one letter to each square, to form words suggested by the trivia clues.

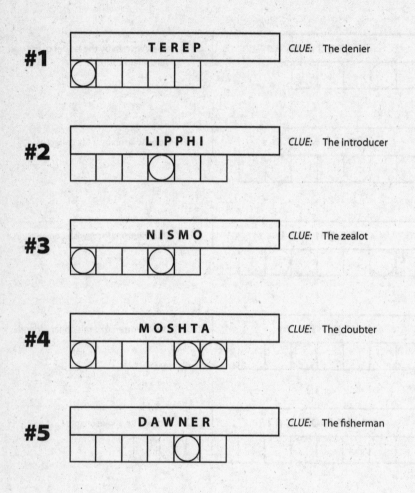

#1 TEREP   CLUE: The denier

#2 LIPPHI   CLUE: The introducer

#3 NISMO   CLUE: The zealot

#4 MOSHTA   CLUE: The doubter

#5 DAWNER   CLUE: The fisherman

Arrange the circled letters to solve the Mystery Answer.

Who were in Jesus' inner circle?

MYSTERY ANSWER:

TRIVIA JUMBLE

Unscramble the Jumbles, one letter to each square, to form words suggested by the trivia clues.

#1 STNIGAPEY
CLUE: Pharaoh's followers

#2 SHASEPIRE
CLUE: New Testament hypocrites

#3 DECUDSEAS
CLUE: Jewish sect

#4 ETOOMINMAPASS
CLUE: Lived between the rivers

#5 BAYSINBOLNA
CLUE: Hammurabi's people

Arrange the circled letters to solve the Mystery Answer.

What do the above names represent?

MYSTERY ANSWER:

TRIVIA JUMBLE

Unscramble the Jumbles, one letter to each square, to form words suggested by the trivia clues.

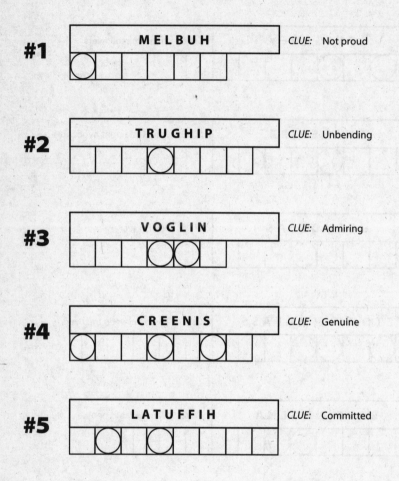

#1 MELBUH CLUE: Not proud

#2 TRUGHIP CLUE: Unbending

#3 VOGLIN CLUE: Admiring

#4 CREENIS CLUE: Genuine

#5 LATUFFIH CLUE: Committed

Arrange the circled letters to solve the Mystery Answer.

What do the above traits summarize?

MYSTERY ANSWER:

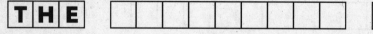

THE ☐☐☐☐☐☐☐☐ LIFE

TRIVIA JUMBLE

Unscramble the Jumbles, one letter to each square, to form words suggested by the trivia clues.

#1 LYGRO — *CLUE:* Heavenly radiance

#2 RILUMCEF — *CLUE:* Kindhearted

#3 DJETMUNG — *CLUE:* Ruling

#4 YEWERVEEHR — *CLUE:* Widely present

#5 MOONSTEPICASA — *CLUE:* Gently sympathetic

Arrange the circled letters to solve the Mystery Answer.

What best reflects the words above?

MYSTERY ANSWER:

TRIVIA JUMBLE

Unscramble the Jumbles, one letter to each square, to form words suggested by the trivia clues.

#1 SIVITHE   CLUE: Descendants of Canaan

#2 SISARSANY   CLUE: Dwellers near the Tigris

#3 TOMARSIE   CLUE: Occupiers west of the Euphrates

#4 KEEMLATISA   CLUE: Children of Esau

#5 ISTETIHT   CLUE: Ancient Anatolians

Arrange the circled letters to solve the Mystery Answer.

What were these nations to Israel?

MYSTERY ANSWER:

TRIVIA JUMBLE

Unscramble the Jumbles, one letter to each square, to form words suggested by the trivia clues.

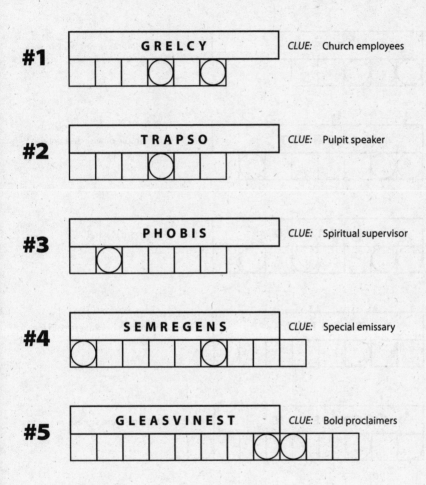

#1 GRELCY — *CLUE:* Church employees

#2 TRAPSO — *CLUE:* Pulpit speaker

#3 PHOBIS — *CLUE:* Spiritual supervisor

#4 SEMREGENS — *CLUE:* Special emissary

#5 GLEASVINEST — *CLUE:* Bold proclaimers

Arrange the circled letters to solve the Mystery Answer.

What common job do each of these offices provide?

MYSTERY ANSWER:

TRIVIA JUMBLE

Unscramble the Jumbles, one letter to each square, to form words suggested by the trivia clues.

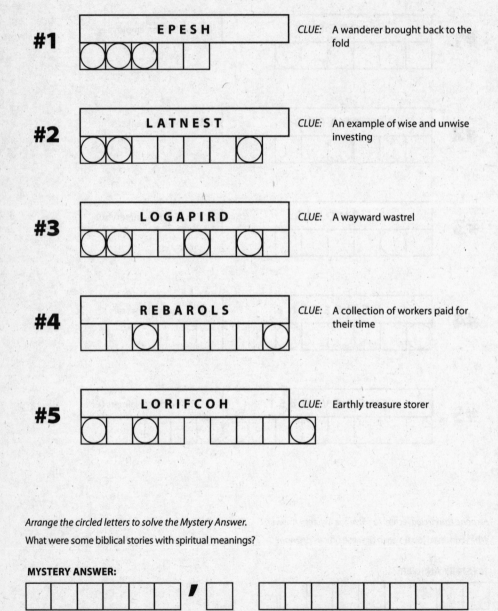

#1 EPESH

CLUE: A wanderer brought back to the fold

#2 LATNEST

CLUE: An example of wise and unwise investing

#3 LOGAPIRD

CLUE: A wayward wastrel

#4 REBAROLS

CLUE: A collection of workers paid for their time

#5 LORIFCOH

CLUE: Earthly treasure storer

Arrange the circled letters to solve the Mystery Answer.

What were some biblical stories with spiritual meanings?

MYSTERY ANSWER:

TRIVIA JUMBLE

Unscramble the Jumbles, one letter to each square, to form words suggested by the trivia clues.

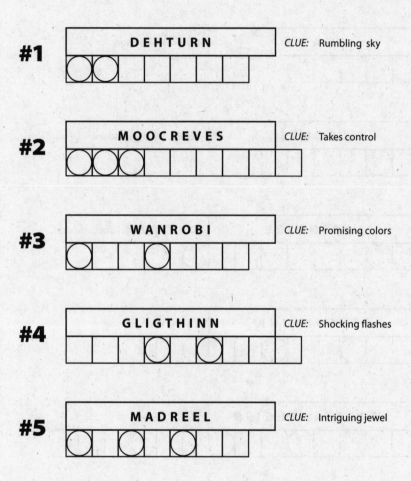

#1 DEHTURN   CLUE: Rumbling sky

#2 MOOCREVES   CLUE: Takes control

#3 WANROBI   CLUE: Promising colors

#4 GLIGTHINN   CLUE: Shocking flashes

#5 MADREEL   CLUE: Intriguing jewel

Arrange the circled letters to solve the Mystery Answer.

Where is God's seat of majesty?

MYSTERY ANSWER:

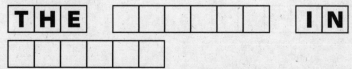

THE ☐☐☐☐☐☐ IN

☐☐☐☐☐☐

TRIVIA JUMBLE

Unscramble the Jumbles, one letter to each square, to form words suggested by the trivia clues.

#1 TRAWH
CLUE: Fierce anger

#2 CRONSS
CLUE: Strongly disdains

#3 LEEBNOIRL
CLUE: Purposeful disobedience

#4 SENSUDNINK
CLUE: Mean attitude

#5 SNORSTANREGISS
CLUE: Lapses

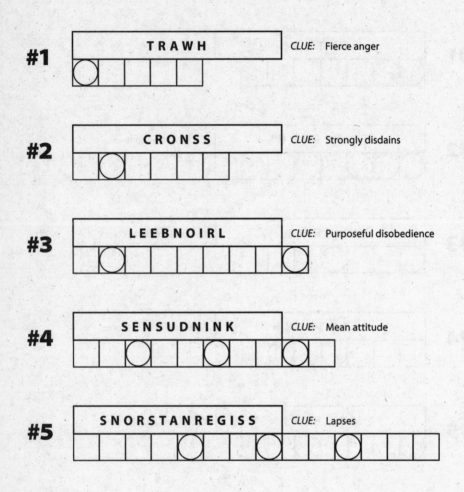

Arrange the circled letters to solve the Mystery Answer.

What does the evil one want to spread?

MYSTERY ANSWER:

TRIVIA JUMBLE

Unscramble the Jumbles, one letter to each square, to form words suggested by the trivia clues.

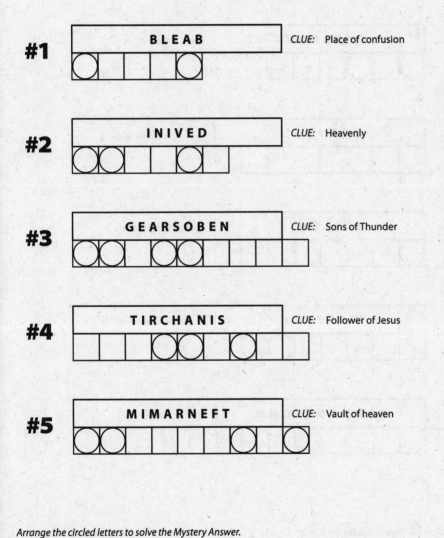

#1 BLEAB CLUE: Place of confusion

#2 INIVED CLUE: Heavenly

#3 GEARSOBEN CLUE: Sons of Thunder

#4 TIRCHANIS CLUE: Follower of Jesus

#5 MIMARNEFT CLUE: Vault of heaven

Arrange the circled letters to solve the Mystery Answer.

What terms do some Bible students learn?

MYSTERY ANSWER:

TRIVIA JUMBLE

Unscramble the Jumbles, one letter to each square, to form words suggested by the trivia clues.

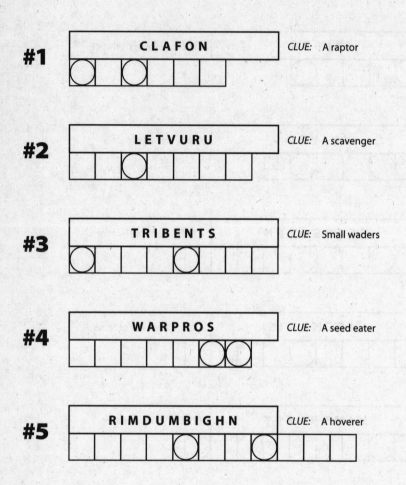

#1 CLAFON CLUE: A raptor

#2 LETVURU CLUE: A scavenger

#3 TRIBENTS CLUE: Small waders

#4 WARPROS CLUE: A seed eater

#5 RIMDUMBIGHN CLUE: A hoverer

Arrange the circled letters to solve the Mystery Answer.

What do the above sky dwellers have in common?

MYSTERY ANSWER:

THEY ARE ☐☐☐☐☐ OF
THE ☐☐☐☐☐

TRIVIA JUMBLE

Unscramble the Jumbles, one letter to each square, to form words suggested by the trivia clues.

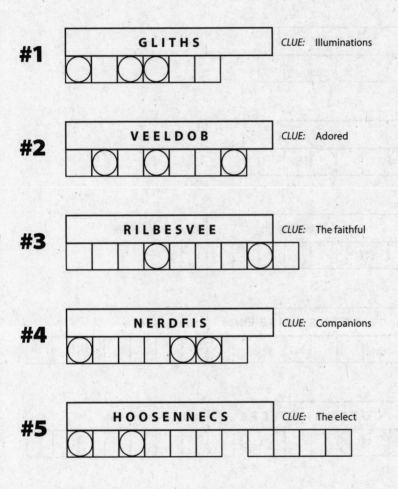

#1 GLITHS CLUE: Illuminations

#2 VEELDOB CLUE: Adored

#3 RILBESVEE CLUE: The faithful

#4 NERDFIS CLUE: Companions

#5 HOOSENNECS CLUE: The elect

Arrange the circled letters to solve the Mystery Answer.

What are the heirs of the heavenly kingdom called?

MYSTERY ANSWER:

TRIVIA JUMBLE

Unscramble the Jumbles, one letter to each square, to form words suggested by the trivia clues.

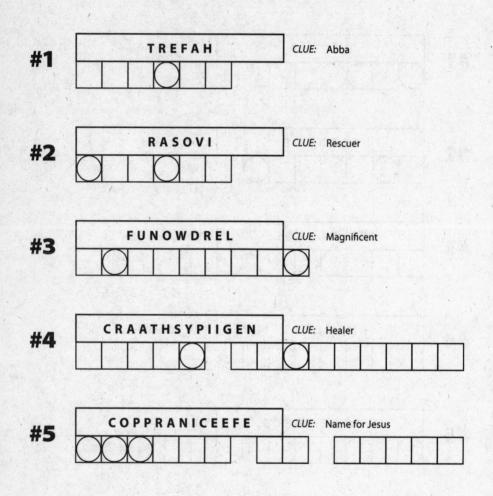

#1 TREFAH   CLUE: Abba

#2 RASOVI   CLUE: Rescuer

#3 FUNOWDREL   CLUE: Magnificent

#4 CRAATHSYPIIGEN   CLUE: Healer

#5 COPPRANICEEFE   CLUE: Name for Jesus

Arrange the circled letters to solve the Mystery Answer.

Which member of the Trinity is featured in the book of Acts?

MYSTERY ANSWER:

TRIVIA JUMBLE

Unscramble the Jumbles, one letter to each square, to form words suggested by the trivia clues.

#1 MEENY   *CLUE:* Foe

#2 PREMETT   *CLUE:* Enticer

#3 SECUCRA   *CLUE:* Finger pointer

#4 YOOLNAPL   *CLUE:* Angel of the bottomless pit

#5 TAFFREEILSOH   *CLUE:* Deceiver

Arrange the circled letters to solve the Mystery Answer.

What do the above words have in common?

MYSTERY ANSWER:

TRIVIA JUMBLE

Unscramble the Jumbles, one letter to each square, to form words suggested by the trivia clues.

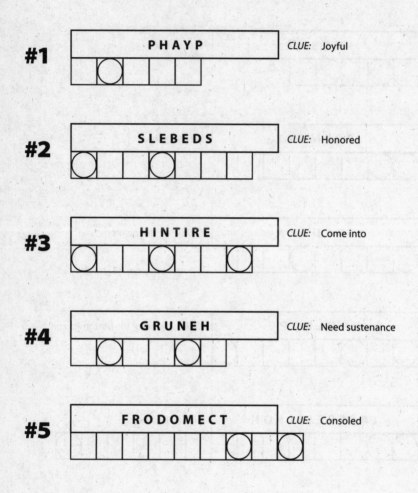

#1 PHAYP — CLUE: Joyful

#2 SLEBEDS — CLUE: Honored

#3 HINTIRE — CLUE: Come into

#4 GRUNEH — CLUE: Need sustenance

#5 FRODOMECT — CLUE: Consoled

Arrange the circled letters to solve the Mystery Answer.

What is the opening part of Jesus' most famous sermon?

MYSTERY ANSWER:

T H E

TRIVIA JUMBLE

Unscramble the Jumbles, one letter to each square, to form words suggested by the trivia clues.

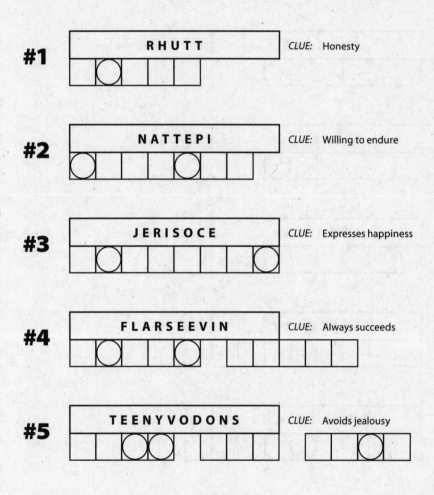

#1 RHUTT CLUE: Honesty

#2 NATTEPI CLUE: Willing to endure

#3 JERISOCE CLUE: Expresses happiness

#4 FLARSEEVIN CLUE: Always succeeds

#5 TEENYVODONS CLUE: Avoids jealousy

Arrange the circled letters to solve the Mystery Answer.

When everything else fails, what does love do?

MYSTERY ANSWER:

L O V E

TRIVIA JUMBLE

Unscramble the Jumbles, one letter to each square, to form words suggested by the trivia clues.

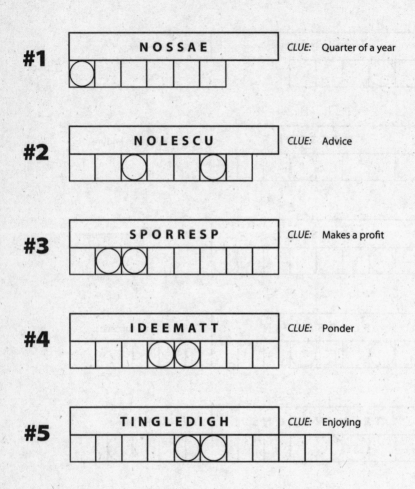

#1 NOSSAE — CLUE: Quarter of a year

#2 NOLESCU — CLUE: Advice

#3 SPORRESP — CLUE: Makes a profit

#4 IDEEMATT — CLUE: Ponder

#5 TINGLEDIGH — CLUE: Enjoying

Arrange the circled letters to solve the Mystery Answer.

According to Psalm 1, what kind of people does the Lord watch over?

MYSTERY ANSWER:

TRIVIA JUMBLE

Unscramble the Jumbles, one letter to each square, to form words suggested by the trivia clues.

#1 MERNSHAD

CLUE: Leads his flocks

#2 ROSSIMINYA

CLUE: Spreads the gospel

#3 PRENCERTA

CLUE: Works with wood

#4 REERPABCU

CLUE: Tests the wine

#5 CALLTOCORTEX

CLUE: Skims the contributions

Arrange the circled letters to solve the Mystery Answer.

In order to provide for themselves and their families, what did the Bible characters need?

MYSTERY ANSWER:

TRIVIA JUMBLE

Unscramble the Jumbles, one letter to each square, to form words suggested by the trivia clues.

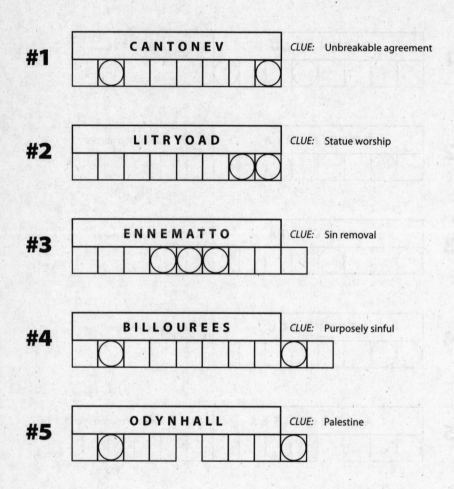

#1 CANTONEV

CLUE: Unbreakable agreement

#2 LITRYOAD

CLUE: Statue worship

#3 ENNEMATTO

CLUE: Sin removal

#4 BILLOUREES

CLUE: Purposely sinful

#5 ODYNHALL

CLUE: Palestine

Arrange the circled letters to solve the Mystery Answer.

What book of the Bible summarizes the three books that come before it?

MYSTERY ANSWER:

TRIVIA JUMBLE

Unscramble the Jumbles, one letter to each square, to form words suggested by the trivia clues.

#1 GESLUPA   *CLUE:* Epidemics

#2 BIRRFOSTN   *CLUE:* Eldest

#3 AHORPAH   *CLUE:* Egyptian

#4 CLOTKIVES   *CLUE:* Animals

#5 SENDRAKS   *CLUE:* Gloom

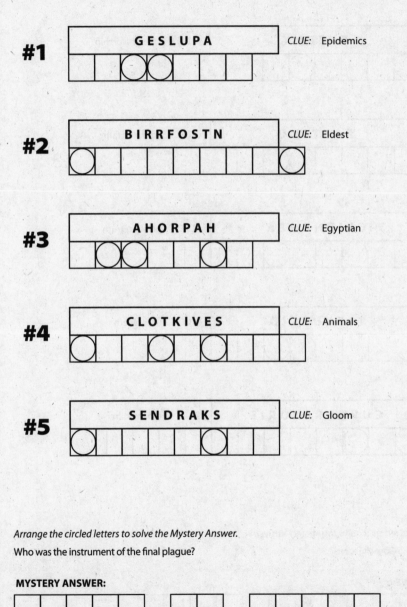

Arrange the circled letters to solve the Mystery Answer.

Who was the instrument of the final plague?

MYSTERY ANSWER:

TRIVIA JUMBLE

Unscramble the Jumbles, one letter to each square, to form words suggested by the trivia clues.

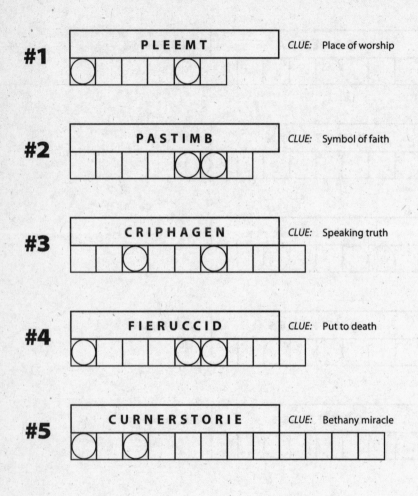

#1 PLEEMT — *CLUE:* Place of worship

#2 PASTIMB — *CLUE:* Symbol of faith

#3 CRIPHAGEN — *CLUE:* Speaking truth

#4 FIERUCCID — *CLUE:* Put to death

#5 CURNERSTORIE — *CLUE:* Bethany miracle

Arrange the circled letters to solve the Mystery Answer.

What events do the Gospels record?

MYSTERY ANSWER:

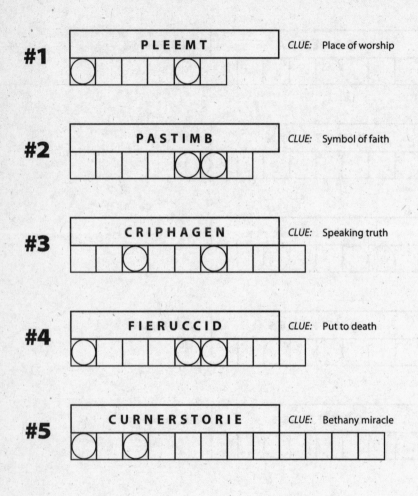

TRIVIA JUMBLE

Unscramble the Jumbles, one letter to each square, to form words suggested by the trivia clues.

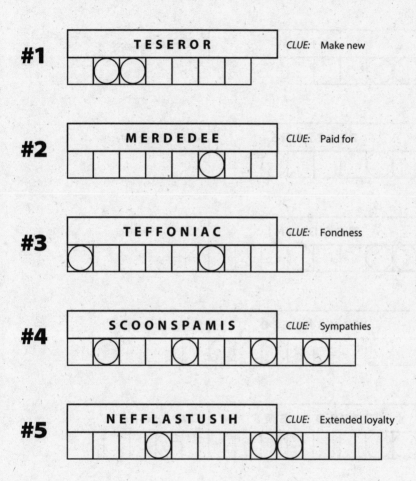

#1 TESEROR — *CLUE:* Make new

#2 MERDEDEE — *CLUE:* Paid for

#3 TEFFONIAC — *CLUE:* Fondness

#4 SCOONSPAMIS — *CLUE:* Sympathies

#5 NEFFLASTUSIH — *CLUE:* Extended loyalty

Arrange the circled letters to solve the Mystery Answer.

What book records Jeremiah's sorrowful poetry?

MYSTERY ANSWER:

TRIVIA JUMBLE

Unscramble the Jumbles, one letter to each square, to form words suggested by the trivia clues.

#1 TRIFU
CLUE: Often sweet

#2 PESTERNS
CLUE: Often scaly

#3 MOODNINI
CLUE: Often kingly

#4 WONGKLEED
CLUE: Often wise

#5 DAVADANEME
CLUE: Often first

Arrange the circled letters to solve the Mystery Answer.

Where did the Fall take place?

MYSTERY ANSWER:

TRIVIA JUMBLE

Unscramble the Jumbles, one letter to each square, to form words suggested by the trivia clues.

#1 RISANDYDONET

CLUE: Region to which Jesus withdrew

#2 TENYBAH

CLUE: Resurrection site

#3 TARZENAH

CLUE: Town where Jesus grew up

#4 CADAMUSS

CLUE: City near Saul's place of conversion

#5 ELEESAGOFALI

CLUE: Stormy lake

Arrange the circled letters to solve the Mystery Answer.

What is another name for Palestine?

MYSTERY ANSWER:

FIND THE JUMBLE
CREATION

Use the clues to help unscramble the Jumbles, one letter to each square, to form ordinary words.

#1 R E E R U T A C S   CLUE: Animals

#2 N O O M I D N I   CLUE: Authority

#3 U F F L T I R U   CLUE: Produces bounty

#4 A O S S N E S   CLUE: Year divisions

#5 N A W M O   CLUE: Female

#6 G E N N I B I N G   CLUE: Start of something

Find and circle the answers (from above) in the grid of letters below.

Z	P	Q	U	H	I	L	C	P	M	Z	N	O	K
C	R	E	A	T	U	R	E	S	C	O	W	J	P
Z	J	N	D	G	N	F	R	U	I	T	F	U	L
W	T	G	Z	A	C	X	T	N	L	Z	D	O	T
C	I	P	M	B	E	G	I	N	N	I	N	G	S
L	V	O	X	U	W	M	T	Y	P	E	A	F	A
V	W	U	N	S	O	D	R	N	U	W	Z	Y	T
Q	G	S	D	D	S	E	A	S	O	N	S	I	J

FIND THE JUMBLE
ACTIONS OF GOD

Use the clues to help unscramble the Jumbles, one letter to each square, to form ordinary words.

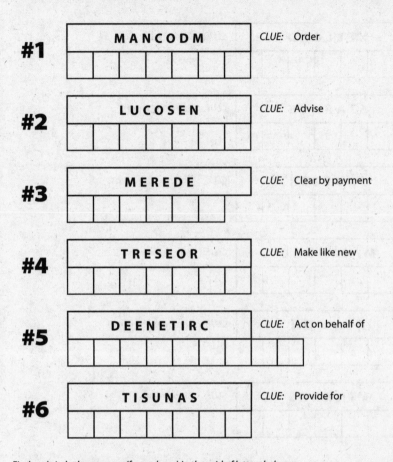

#1 MANCODM — CLUE: Order

#2 LUCOSEN — CLUE: Advise

#3 MEREDE — CLUE: Clear by payment

#4 TRESEOR — CLUE: Make like new

#5 DEENETIRC — CLUE: Act on behalf of

#6 TISUNAS — CLUE: Provide for

Find and circle the answers (from above) in the grid of letters below.

S	C	O	U	N	S	E	L	T	E	U	X	Q	Q
Z	U	Y	F	D	Z	B	U	A	T	S	F	D	X
T	Q	S	I	N	T	E	R	C	E	D	E	A	K
V	W	H	T	K	J	H	E	P	E	W	N	R	J
C	O	M	M	A	N	D	D	K	Z	H	D	Z	C
Q	B	M	L	H	I	R	E	S	T	O	R	E	I
I	W	Y	B	Z	M	N	E	B	G	U	S	F	E
H	F	H	P	P	J	G	M	E	E	F	U	M	D

FIND THE JUMBLE
RUTH

Use the clues to help unscramble the Jumbles, one letter to each square, to form ordinary words.

#1   N E E L G A D   CLUE: Gathered

#2   S T A R H V E   CLUE: Farmer's bounty

#3   S A R P E E R   CLUE: Collectors of crops

#4   M I N A H D A D   CLUE: Female servant

#5   N I W W O N   CLUE: Separate from chaff

#6   M I N K A N S   CLUE: Blood relative

Find and circle the answers (from above) in the grid of letters below.

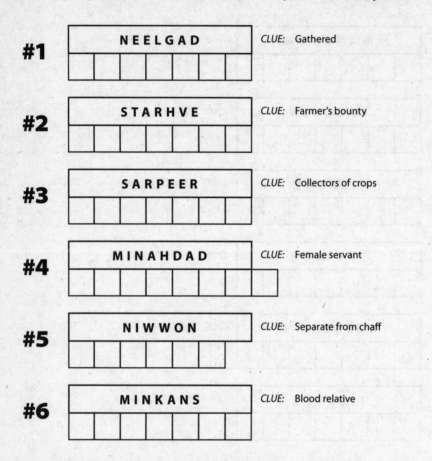

H	W	T	Y	K	I	N	S	M	A	N	B	J	Z
A	O	S	X	Q	Z	G	M	C	M	Z	A	X	I
R	N	V	W	O	G	L	L	T	Q	Q	R	Z	E
V	O	V	D	F	U	I	S	E	N	R	L	U	L
E	H	A	N	D	M	A	I	D	A	G	R	B	R
S	R	M	C	N	D	Z	W	I	N	N	O	W	U
T	X	F	S	R	E	A	P	E	R	S	E	F	G
L	P	W	O	N	A	F	Q	W	D	Y	J	D	O

178

FIND THE JUMBLE
JONAH

Use the clues to help unscramble the Jumbles, one letter to each square, to form ordinary words.

#1 NAJHO — *CLUE:* Fishy prophet

#2 VEENNHI — *CLUE:* Assyrian capital

#3 THIRSAHS — *CLUE:* Ancient country

#4 STIRDSES — *CLUE:* Anxiety

#5 PAPJO — *CLUE:* Seaside town

#6 RYPEAR — *CLUE:* Conversation with God

Find and circle the answers (from above) in the grid of letters below.

Y	W	J	M	P	R	A	Y	E	R	J	D	W	Q
W	Q	D	O	H	J	N	G	G	W	U	M	O	Z
Y	T	V	A	P	E	A	I	O	V	F	U	B	Y
V	P	N	W	A	P	X	M	N	T	X	Y	U	T
F	O	G	U	K	P	A	F	I	E	N	W	B	U
J	T	A	R	S	H	I	S	H	V	V	V	S	O
Q	F	O	U	Y	G	D	I	S	T	R	E	S	S
Q	O	Y	E	D	B	C	I	C	B	I	E	H	K

FIND THE JUMBLE
FIRST KINGS

Use the clues to help unscramble the Jumbles, one letter to each square, to form ordinary words.

#1 MOOLSNO — CLUE: Wealthy king of Israel

#2 MOWSID — CLUE: Discernment

#3 METELP — CLUE: House of worship

#4 CALEPA — CLUE: Royal residence

#5 GNOKIMD — CLUE: Territory

#6 VADDI — CLUE: Second king

Find and circle the answers (from above) in the grid of letters below.

```
K O X D G R M D E Y B G T Y
I U V Q B O B L X R A N O T
N P O H D R P E Z M F E Q A
G L U S D M C Z A O S I G P
D U I R E A S O L O M O N A
O W O T L A V M S S O K N D
M W I A L I V I T U J E X N
Q S P L D X G J D D R P K H
```

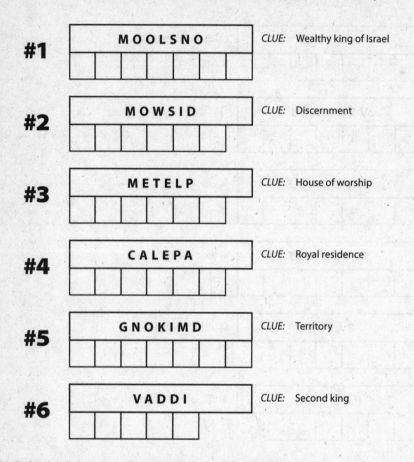

FIND THE JUMBLE

EXODUS

Use the clues to help unscramble the Jumbles, one letter to each square, to form ordinary words.

#1 LUIQA — CLUE: Migratory game bird

#2 ANNMA — CLUE: Bread from heaven

#3 LUGGINBRM — CLUE: Complaining

#4 TRAWE — CLUE: Desert need

#5 FAFST — CLUE: Rod

#6 GRINSPS — CLUE: Flowing streams

Find and circle the answers (from above) in the grid of letters below.

Z	W	M	V	N	M	C	A	F	A	D	A	C	G
B	Q	U	A	I	L	S	F	A	I	N	W	F	D
S	D	N	D	H	I	A	C	Y	N	J	W	W	Q
X	S	K	W	A	T	E	R	A	M	A	J	D	R
A	J	J	D	S	W	A	M	M	Q	X	P	J	W
R	C	Q	S	P	R	I	N	G	S	L	Y	X	Z
I	U	P	I	G	Y	P	Z	T	G	L	E	Y	B
K	B	U	Z	G	R	U	M	B	L	I	N	G	Z

FIND THE JUMBLE
BIBLE GENRES

Use the clues to help unscramble the Jumbles, one letter to each square, to form ordinary words.

#1 B A A R L E P   CLUE: Illustrative story

#2 C R O A L E   CLUE: Balaam's utterance

#3 P Y R O P E C H   CLUE: Direction from God

#4 P L E G O S   CLUE: Biography of Jesus

#5 T E E L I P S   CLUE: Paul's letter

#6 L O A G R E Y L   CLUE: Symbolic narrative

Find and circle the answers (from above) in the grid of letters below.

K	Y	O	I	A	G	V	G	H	J	O	L	F	D
S	O	O	I	P	R	O	P	H	E	C	Y	O	A
P	A	R	A	B	L	E	G	K	I	P	T	H	H
K	I	A	A	Y	E	U	S	O	Z	N	U	Z	W
M	J	C	A	G	C	E	P	I	S	T	L	E	K
R	A	L	L	E	G	O	R	Y	T	P	P	A	R
B	X	E	Z	K	F	D	V	K	R	H	E	E	X
L	G	I	J	V	A	R	H	O	G	U	O	L	B

182

FIND THE JUMBLE
SINS AND SHORTCOMINGS

Use the clues to help unscramble the Jumbles, one letter to each square, to form ordinary words.

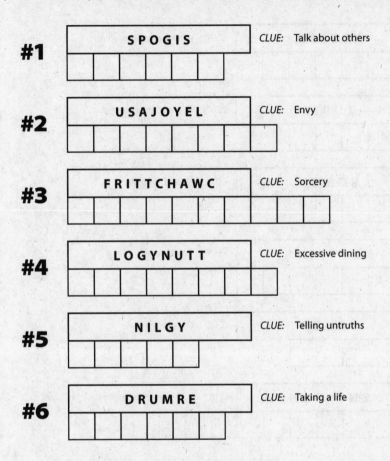

#1 SPOGIS

CLUE: Talk about others

#2 USAJOYEL

CLUE: Envy

#3 FRITTCHAWC

CLUE: Sorcery

#4 LOGYNUTT

CLUE: Excessive dining

#5 NILGY

CLUE: Telling untruths

#6 DRUMRE

CLUE: Taking a life

Find and circle the answers (from above) in the grid of letters below.

I	V	J	E	A	L	O	U	S	Y	Y	L	P	O
J	K	M	B	K	V	N	V	I	V	C	I	K	X
T	G	L	U	T	T	O	N	Y	Y	S	D	C	X
H	D	C	V	R	W	L	O	E	S	K	A	A	D
G	M	P	M	C	D	K	Y	O	B	A	N	V	J
F	D	A	F	K	E	E	G	I	Y	N	I	E	X
W	J	I	B	T	W	D	R	R	N	O	P	N	F
W	I	T	C	H	C	R	A	F	T	G	E	B	M

183

FIND THE JUMBLE
MEASUREMENTS

Use the clues to help unscramble the Jumbles, one letter to each square, to form ordinary words.

#1 KEELSH   CLUE: Ancient monetary unit

#2 TUBIC   CLUE: Forearm measurement

#3 ROMEH   CLUE: Unit of capacity

#4 NURSIEDA   CLUE: Day's wage

#5 PAHEH   CLUE: Dry measure

#6 DHENTABAHRD   CLUE: Linear measurement

Find and circle the answers (from above) in the grid of letters below.

F	S	D	U	C	T	H	F	B	S	D	U	J	S
S	U	E	P	H	A	H	O	U	F	R	E	Z	U
H	S	N	P	E	R	S	X	M	J	M	A	E	O
E	B	A	H	A	N	D	B	R	E	A	D	T	H
K	C	R	O	C	P	E	R	H	V	R	K	U	E
E	V	I	V	O	C	N	I	Z	P	W	W	U	F
L	E	U	J	B	M	A	C	U	B	I	T	O	J
X	O	S	G	U	F	C	K	Y	H	J	A	V	W

184

FIND THE JUMBLE
CITIES

Use the clues to help unscramble the Jumbles, one letter to each square, to form ordinary words.

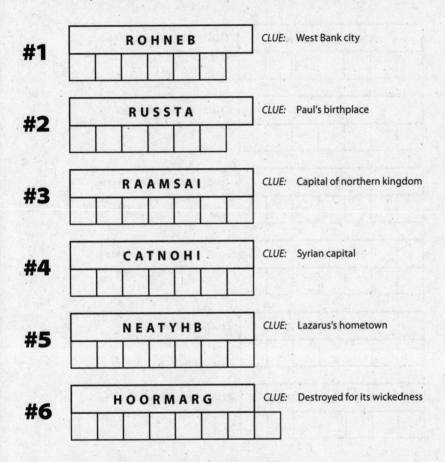

#1 ROHNEB   CLUE: West Bank city

#2 RUSSTA   CLUE: Paul's birthplace

#3 RAAMSAI   CLUE: Capital of northern kingdom

#4 CATNOHI   CLUE: Syrian capital

#5 NEATYHB   CLUE: Lazarus's hometown

#6 HOORMARG   CLUE: Destroyed for its wickedness

Find and circle the answers (from above) in the grid of letters below.

F	Q	R	D	F	N	H	A	Z	P	O	R	Y	Q
E	N	S	P	O	C	U	B	L	E	L	R	N	Y
A	L	H	A	O	D	S	T	Z	K	Y	M	N	N
D	Z	R	I	M	G	O	M	O	R	R	A	H	R
H	J	T	M	B	A	G	E	T	U	H	K	J	Q
V	N	Z	H	E	B	R	O	N	T	H	E	K	D
A	O	A	P	E	N	L	I	E	W	N	W	M	Y
T	A	R	S	U	S	S	B	A	F	H	F	Y	I

FIND THE JUMBLE
BIBLE HEROES

Use the clues to help unscramble the Jumbles, one letter to each square, to form ordinary words.

#1 | R A B B A S A N | **CLUE:** Contemporary of Paul

#2 | A R U L S Z A | **CLUE:** Received a miracle

#3 | J E L H A I | **CLUE:** Old Testament prophet

#4 | H O T R E J | **CLUE:** Father-in-law of Moses

#5 | R O O M B E J A | **CLUE:** Rebel leader

#6 | M O H L I N E P | **CLUE:** Letter recipient

Find and circle the answers (from above) in the grid of letters below.

C	U	W	E	L	I	J	A	H	M	N	Z	D	S
J	M	P	T	J	I	E	C	A	O	A	Y	U	N
D	E	D	G	Y	J	K	O	M	T	R	R	J	F
F	Y	T	V	N	N	B	E	X	T	A	A	X	R
E	G	G	H	Z	O	L	N	F	Z	T	Z	D	T
R	N	O	U	R	I	G	G	A	U	L	Y	E	G
M	Q	Q	E	H	O	H	L	Y	D	F	K	I	M
A	C	J	P	B	A	R	N	A	B	A	S	M	Z

FIND THE JUMBLE
CRUCIFIXION

Use the clues to help unscramble the Jumbles, one letter to each square, to form ordinary words.

#1 SAJDU CLUE: Traitor

#2 YATREBLA CLUE: Treason

#3 RUTTOER CLUE: Inflict pain

#4 CROMKEY CLUE: Making fun

#5 RAADIPES CLUE: Heavenly place

#6 FEHTI CLUE: Crook

Find and circle the answers (from above) in the grid of letters below.

B	E	T	R	A	Y	A	L	F	E	R	B	I	E
L	O	T	M	L	U	B	A	S	Y	J	T	R	V
A	J	Y	S	J	E	T	I	Q	B	D	U	M	U
E	J	Y	J	C	K	D	H	P	G	T	A	Z	C
B	F	N	U	J	A	S	V	I	R	N	Y	E	P
X	B	D	D	R	M	B	U	O	E	R	T	Q	U
Z	H	X	A	M	J	Q	T	U	I	F	G	I	M
T	P	P	S	M	O	C	K	E	R	Y	V	M	U

187

FIND THE JUMBLE
JESUS IN THE BOAT

Use the clues to help unscramble the Jumbles, one letter to each square, to form ordinary words.

#1 LASLUQ CLUE: Sudden storm

#2 WESVA CLUE: Rippled water

#3 TIFHA CLUE: Belief without sight

#4 CLISSPEDI CLUE: Followers

#5 KEERBU CLUE: Reprimand

#6 DRAAFI CLUE: Filled with fear

Find and circle the answers (from above) in the grid of letters below.

Q	O	N	I	B	N	H	N	O	X	E	Q	Z	Q
N	K	D	G	O	E	W	A	V	E	S	D	Z	F
L	D	K	H	K	V	D	D	G	T	T	Z	C	S
C	K	B	U	V	M	I	V	E	D	Q	G	N	G
R	L	B	D	I	A	V	V	D	M	V	V	N	D
G	E	N	F	R	W	H	M	R	V	D	E	C	L
R	C	V	F	D	I	S	C	I	P	L	E	S	S
G	F	A	I	T	H	Z	S	Q	U	A	L	L	R

FIND THE JUMBLE
FEEDING THE FIVE THOUSAND

Use the clues to help unscramble the Jumbles, one letter to each square, to form ordinary words.

#1 DWORC   *CLUE:* Large gathering

#2 SARGS   *CLUE:* Ground covering

#3 ALVOSE   *CLUE:* Bakery units

#4 TESSBAK   *CLUE:* Woven containers

#5 IDAFETISS   *CLUE:* Sated

#6 PILLMETDIU   *CLUE:* Increased significantly

Find and circle the answers (from above) in the grid of letters below.

W	B	K	Z	S	A	T	I	S	F	I	E	D	W
Q	V	A	M	E	D	P	E	P	J	Y	B	G	O
M	D	C	S	W	J	V	T	P	I	I	Y	U	O
X	E	B	O	K	A	A	G	I	S	Q	F	V	D
A	P	R	B	O	E	K	V	R	T	N	E	U	Y
A	C	V	L	X	I	T	O	S	A	E	V	X	D
S	Q	C	P	L	B	F	S	P	G	S	U	A	R
L	M	U	L	T	I	P	L	I	E	D	S	Z	Y

FIND THE JUMBLE
NAMES OF JESUS

Use the clues to help unscramble the Jumbles, one letter to each square, to form ordinary words.

#1   N E I L M U M A   CLUE: "God is with us"

#2   O H A V E J H   CLUE: "God of deliverance"

#3   S A S H E M I   CLUE: Anticipated Savior

#4   K F K G S O I N G N I   CLUE: Chief ruler

#5   L O O S C E R U N   CLUE: Adviser

#6   G I Y M H A T L   CLUE: powerful

Find and circle the answers (from above) in the grid of letters below.

J	G	I	I	B	X	M	A	N	B	X	L	G	K
E	D	K	U	X	E	L	M	H	B	E	Z	L	S
H	N	D	Q	S	M	E	L	X	U	M	K	I	J
O	H	F	S	I	C	O	U	N	S	E	L	O	R
V	L	I	G	K	Y	W	A	E	K	G	P	R	V
A	A	H	U	L	Z	M	U	S	C	E	I	D	Z
H	T	V	W	T	M	J	J	T	U	E	V	A	C
Y	O	R	K	I	N	G	O	F	K	I	N	G	S

FIND THE JUMBLE
WOMEN OF THE BIBLE

Use the clues to help unscramble the Jumbles, one letter to each square, to form ordinary words.

#1 RAHMTA   *CLUE:* Sister of Lazarus

#2 NAANHH   *CLUE:* Mother of Samuel

#3 TEELZHIBA   *CLUE:* Wife of Zechariah

#4 CEENUI   *CLUE:* Mother of Timothy

#5 GRAAH   *CLUE:* Mother of Ishmael

#6 LAMOSE   *CLUE:* Tomb visitor

Find and circle the answers (from above) in the grid of letters below.

E	L	I	Z	A	B	E	T	H	V	G	O	J	G
D	S	H	W	Z	U	E	I	W	S	M	I	T	M
M	H	L	X	G	O	L	U	V	O	A	F	E	E
W	E	D	X	Y	P	H	D	N	H	K	M	O	S
H	A	N	N	A	H	A	G	T	I	O	U	V	V
I	X	R	N	F	P	G	R	X	L	C	F	E	P
Z	L	T	A	X	A	A	U	A	E	N	E	Y	B
Q	X	N	W	B	M	R	S	B	W	H	R	I	F

FIND THE JUMBLE
OLD TESTAMENT BOOKS

Use the clues to help unscramble the Jumbles, one letter to each square, to form ordinary words.

#1 MALPSS — CLUE: Book of prayers

#2 KEEZLIE — CLUE: Major prophet

#3 BORRVESP — CLUE: Book of wisdom

#4 HOUJAS — CLUE: Conquering Canaan

#5 LECCONSHIR — CLUE: Book of records

#6 HAISIA — CLUE: Spoke of the coming Messiah

Find and circle the answers (from above) in the grid of letters below.

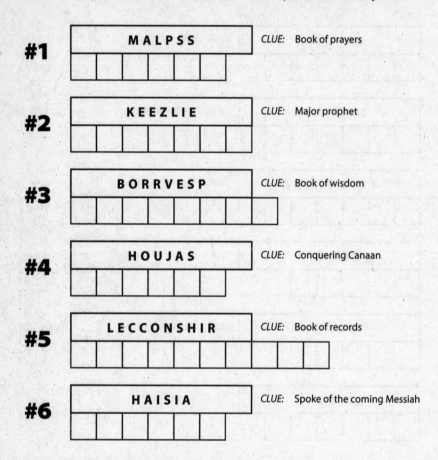

```
C V Q K B I P R I H L D U G
P S A L M S R F D E L A V Q
P Y M C H R O N I C L E S P
X P W B D S V K T P Z U V J
M C K L B T E W L Z R I D K
I S L I A Z R I S A I A H E
H U L Z E D B Y J L D W B J
Y F Y Y J O S H U A K Y B G
```

FIND THE JUMBLE
NEW TESTAMENT

Use the clues to help unscramble the Jumbles, one letter to each square, to form ordinary words.

#1 MOPSTA — CLUE: Island of exile

#2 TOYMIHT — CLUE: Young friend of Paul

#3 ENJOYUR — CLUE: Voyage

#4 NORPIS — CLUE: Jail

#5 WEERSHB — CLUE: Israelites

#6 GARUCEO — CLUE: Bravery

Find and circle the answers (from above) in the grid of letters below.

W	F	N	U	P	W	I	I	A	Y	W	Y	I	E
U	J	U	U	N	A	N	W	M	D	H	F	J	D
T	O	Y	Z	C	W	T	C	U	T	J	R	F	U
S	U	Y	J	S	L	C	M	O	B	N	C	H	D
P	R	I	S	O	N	R	M	O	L	Y	Y	Z	J
D	N	E	Q	W	X	I	Y	U	S	M	I	L	D
H	E	U	K	L	T	D	C	O	U	R	A	G	E
X	Y	H	E	B	R	E	W	S	J	Y	S	L	G

FIND THE JUMBLE
VILLAINS OF THE BIBLE

Use the clues to help unscramble the Jumbles, one letter to each square, to form ordinary words.

#1 HOTLAGI — CLUE: Big Philistine

#2 HILLEAD — CLUE: Lured Samson

#3 SABARBAB — CLUE: Pardoned from execution

#4 INSAANA — CLUE: Destroyed for his dishonesty

#5 SILKUGNA — CLUE: Sought David's life

#6 RAHOPAH — CLUE: Had a hard heart

Find and circle the answers (from above) in the grid of letters below.

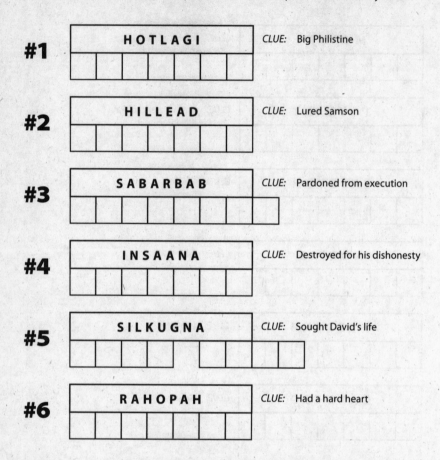

B	L	K	F	O	P	Q	F	Q	M	L	R	A	U
A	S	S	A	Z	H	B	F	R	R	E	F	J	Y
R	G	O	L	I	A	T	H	L	O	C	L	E	U
A	X	Z	S	L	R	C	R	D	N	E	G	Q	B
B	E	Z	Y	W	A	K	I	N	G	S	A	U	L
B	M	F	L	U	O	I	V	B	U	U	E	P	M
A	N	M	L	G	H	D	E	L	I	L	A	H	A
S	F	E	A	N	A	N	I	A	S	K	D	E	A

FIND THE JUMBLE
FRUIT OF THE SPIRIT

Use the clues to help unscramble the Jumbles, one letter to each square, to form ordinary words.

#1 E C A P E   *CLUE:* Calmness of spirit

#2 C A N E P E T I   *CLUE:* Ability to wait

#3 G L E N S E N T E S   *CLUE:* Tender actions

#4 S N O O D G E S   *CLUE:* Honorable actions

#5 R O L L T O F S C E N   *CLUE:* Restraint

#6 D E N N S I K S   *CLUE:* Friendly actions

Find and circle the answers (from above) in the grid of letters below.

T	G	E	N	T	L	E	N	E	S	S	M	V	E
O	S	E	L	F	C	O	N	T	R	O	L	C	N
N	E	P	V	A	Q	B	U	V	T	J	N	W	X
L	S	F	E	E	G	O	O	D	N	E	S	S	Y
P	A	P	H	E	J	E	F	M	I	T	Z	B	S
K	I	N	D	N	E	S	S	T	M	Z	V	C	N
Z	A	Y	I	U	Z	C	A	B	Y	E	P	X	K
R	B	B	Q	R	V	P	N	E	U	Y	B	L	U

195

FIND THE JUMBLE
ATTRIBUTES OF GOD

Use the clues to help unscramble the Jumbles, one letter to each square, to form ordinary words.

#1 NASVIG   CLUE: Rescuing

#2 MONNISTICE   CLUE: All-knowing

#3 FLIGREDIO   CLUE: Covered in majesty

#4 JEDUG   CLUE: Arbiter

#5 SOURGAIC   CLUE: Passing on judgment

#6 VINIFROGG   CLUE: Dismissing of sin

Find and circle the answers (from above) in the grid of letters below.

O	M	N	I	S	C	I	E	N	T	N	P	F	R
M	B	E	N	V	K	K	Q	X	J	G	A	H	E
B	K	B	O	S	D	Z	J	Z	N	G	R	E	C
S	H	X	J	F	O	R	G	I	V	I	N	G	K
X	K	U	N	U	X	B	V	C	M	E	N	C	I
U	V	H	K	Y	D	A	Q	T	R	L	L	Q	R
Z	B	Q	A	J	S	G	R	A	C	I	O	U	S
G	L	O	R	I	F	I	E	D	Q	G	J	R	T

196

FIND THE JUMBLE
NOAH'S ARK

Use the clues to help unscramble the Jumbles, one letter to each square, to form ordinary words.

#1 VOCATENN   *CLUE:* Agreement

#2 DOLFO   *CLUE:* Destroying water

#3 SAPRI   *CLUE:* Groups of two

#4 NORIBWA   *CLUE:* Multicolored band

#5 YIFMAL   *CLUE:* Relatives

#6 SYRPSEC   *CLUE:* Tree species

Find and circle the answers (from above) in the grid of letters below.

F	I	A	C	P	C	D	U	X	W	K	M	V	V
A	T	E	A	Z	O	O	K	F	S	K	Z	W	W
M	E	K	P	O	B	C	V	T	C	O	O	Z	B
I	P	J	L	B	X	B	O	E	V	B	B	R	I
L	K	F	C	M	J	O	M	P	N	N	L	J	W
Y	C	Y	P	R	E	S	S	I	S	A	W	Z	H
A	V	Z	V	H	V	P	A	I	R	S	N	P	J
G	Z	X	S	Z	Y	R	L	I	C	K	N	T	Q

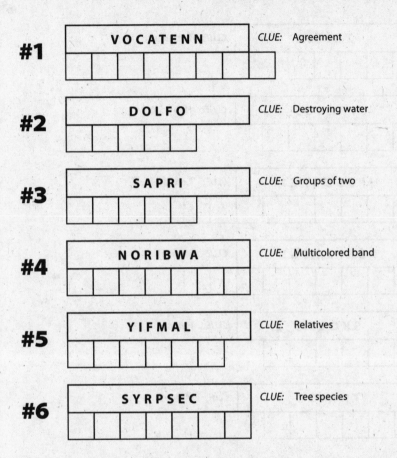

197

FIND THE JUMBLE
CHRISTMAS

Use the clues to help unscramble the Jumbles, one letter to each square, to form ordinary words.

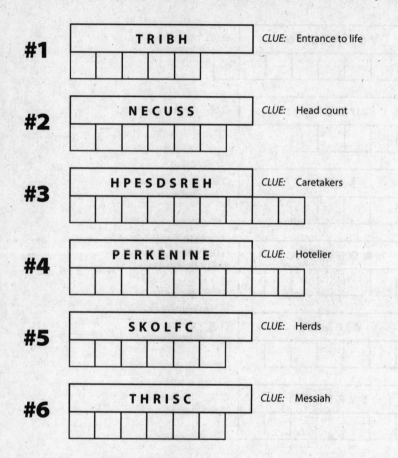

#1   T R I B H   CLUE: Entrance to life

#2   N E C U S S   CLUE: Head count

#3   H P E S D S R E H   CLUE: Caretakers

#4   P E R K E N I N E   CLUE: Hotelier

#5   S K O L F C   CLUE: Herds

#6   T H R I S C   CLUE: Messiah

Find and circle the answers (from above) in the grid of letters below.

C	S	O	X	Q	H	A	Z	O	W	Q	F	C	M
E	M	J	C	T	I	N	N	K	E	E	P	E	R
X	E	O	R	H	K	Z	L	O	T	Y	T	J	Y
X	D	I	S	O	R	F	L	O	C	K	S	G	I
F	B	B	U	H	T	I	O	X	C	E	N	X	L
C	E	N	S	U	S	V	S	O	Z	N	J	M	K
U	I	S	X	W	Q	R	C	T	D	H	I	C	Y
R	F	S	D	R	E	H	P	E	H	S	B	Q	T

FIND THE JUMBLE
BIBLE OBJECTS

Use the clues to help unscramble the Jumbles, one letter to each square, to form ordinary words.

#1   L A M E C S   CLUE: Desert dwellers

#2   C L U B L O S K   CLUE: Steers

#3   E S S E E C H   CLUE: Dairy products

#4   T O R S I H A C   CLUE: Horse-drawn vehicles

#5   S L I P R A L   CLUE: Columns

#6   N U T A R I C S   CLUE: Draperies

Find and circle the answers (from above) in the grid of letters below.

B	D	L	V	H	V	S	X	R	R	X	T	B	C
U	U	I	Z	N	R	F	C	V	H	A	U	Y	A
M	G	L	T	A	C	Q	C	H	E	E	S	E	S
O	C	J	L	C	H	A	R	I	O	T	S	X	G
N	P	L	N	O	W	D	M	J	F	K	I	B	J
E	I	Z	V	Z	C	V	H	E	X	S	Z	T	K
P	T	K	H	W	Z	K	M	F	L	X	W	B	F
C	U	R	T	A	I	N	S	S	J	S	B	G	S

FIND THE JUMBLE
PARABLES

Use the clues to help unscramble the Jumbles, one letter to each square, to form ordinary words.

#1 ETTLANS — CLUE: Units of measure

#2 DUPNOS — CLUE: Currency or weights

#3 DIWOW — CLUE: Surviving spouse

#4 BRESLOAR — CLUE: Workers

#5 EURRESTA — CLUE: Value

#6 IREFGET — CLUE: Withered plant

Find and circle the answers (from above) in the grid of letters below.

T	Y	X	Y	L	O	R	I	I	D	D	C	O	S
F	Q	T	E	S	A	T	R	E	A	S	U	R	E
I	W	Q	T	W	Q	B	L	S	P	F	K	F	O
G	Y	X	V	I	F	M	O	S	O	T	B	X	F
T	N	Z	V	D	V	K	P	R	Q	M	W	F	H
R	E	Z	P	O	U	N	D	S	E	E	O	J	B
E	J	C	M	W	N	P	H	V	R	R	A	Y	E
E	G	T	A	L	E	N	T	S	Z	A	S	C	L

ANSWERS

JUMBLES

1. **Jumbles:** 1. CUBIT | 2. CANDLESTICKS | 3. SHEKELS | 4. PILLARS | 5. COMMANDMENTS
   Mystery Answer: SETS [OF] TEN

2. **Jumbles:** 1. UNENDING | 2. MERCIFUL | 3. RIGHTEOUS | 4. OMNISCIENT | 5. COMPASSION
   Mystery Answer: INFINITE

3. **Jumbles:** 1. PHILISTINES | 2. CANAANITES | 3. AMALEKITES | 4. EGYPTIANS | 5. AMORITES
   Mystery Answer: ISRAEL['] S ENEMIES

4. **Jumbles:** 1. ARARAT | 2. SINAI | 3. OLIVES | 4. HERMON | 5. OLYMPUS
   Mystery Answer: MOUNTAINS

5. **Jumbles:** 1. DONKEYS | 2. SHEEP | 3. CAMELS | 4. IGUANAS | 5. LEOPARDS
   Mystery Answer: ANIMALS

6. **Jumbles:** 1. PARTRIDGE | 2. SPARROW | 3. FALCON | 4. BITTERN | 5. NIGHTHAWK
   Mystery Answer: BIRDS [OF THE] AIR

7. **Jumbles:** 1. SIMON PETER | 2. ANDREW | 3. THADDEUS | 4. PHILIP | 5. ISCARIOT
   Mystery Answer: CHOSEN

8. **Jumbles:** 1. CENTURION | 2. FISHERMAN | 3. CARPENTER | 4. PROPHET | 5. SERVANT
   Mystery Answer: MERCHANT

9. **Jumbles:** 1. SOLOMON | 2. PAUL | 3. OBADIAH | 4. JEREMIAH | 5. MATTHEW
   Mystery Answer: AUTHORS

10. **Jumbles:** 1. HEBREWS | 2. REVELATION | 3. THIRD JOHN | 4. FIRST PETER | 5. PHILEMON
    Mystery Answer: EPHESIANS

11. **Jumbles:** 1. GARMENTS | 2. MERCIES | 3. COVENANT | 4. WONDERS | 5. HEAVENS
    Mystery Answer: NEW THINGS

12. **Jumbles:** 1. MOABITESS | 2. COVERING | 3. JUDAH | 4. KINSMAN | 5. HANDMAID
    Mystery Answer: RUTH [AND] NAOMI

13. **Jumbles:** 1. REDEEMER | 2. TRINITY | 3. INTERCESSOR | 4. GOVERNOR | 5. COMPASSIONATE
    Mystery Answer: DIVINITY

14. **Jumbles:** 1. ASAPH | 2. LEVITES | 3. SANBALLAT | 4. HISTORY | 5. CAPTIVITY
    Mystery Answer: TOBIAH

15. **Jumbles:** 1. PROPHECY | 2. TRUTHFUL | 3. COUNSELOR | 4. GLORIOUS | 5. ADVOCATE
    Mystery Answer: HOLY GHOST

16. **Jumbles:** 1. PREACHER | 2. PASTOR | 3. EVANGELIST | 4. MESSENGER | 5. BISHOP
    Mystery Answer: MINISTERS

17. **Jumbles:** 1. SAVIOR | 2. MAGI | 3. NIGHT SKY | 4. MYRRH | 5. BETHLEHEM
    Mystery Answer: NATIVITY

18. **Jumbles:** 1. PEACE | 2. IMMANUEL | 3. SHEPHERDS | 4. CRECHE | 5. TAXING
    Mystery Answer: MANGER

19. **Jumbles:** 1. IMAGE | 2. DOMINION | 3. BEGINNING | 4. FRUITFUL | 5. CATTLE
    Mystery Answer: CREATION

20. **Jumbles:** 1. JERUSALEM | 2. SYRIA | 3. MACEDONIA | 4. DAMASCUS | 5. PTOLEMAIS
    Mystery Answer: PAUL['] S JOURNEYS

21. **Jumbles:** 1. WONDERFUL | 2. MESSIAH | 3. FAITHFUL | 4. PRINCE OF PEACE | 5. ADVOCATE
    Mystery Answer: CHIEF CORNERSTONE

22. **Jumbles:** 1. SIXTH HOUR | 2. CENTURION | 3. PILATE | 4. VILIFY | 5. CAIAPHAS
    Mystery Answer: CRUCIFY

23. **Jumbles:** 1. PRODIGAL | 2. BRANCHES | 3. LABORERS | 4. TALENTS | 5. SEEDS
    Mystery Answer: PARABLES

24. **Jumbles:** 1. EXILED | 2. PHARAOH | 3. EGYPTIAN | 4. DEUTERONOMY | 5. LEVITICUS
    Mystery Answer: EXODUS

25. **Jumbles:** 1. EPHESIANS | 2. COLOSSIANS | 3. TITUS | 4. CORINTHIANS | 5. GALATIANS
    Mystery Answer: EPISTLES

26. **Jumbles:** 2A. FOCUS | 5A. BURSTING | 6A. YOUNGER | 7A. CHERRIES | 1D. HOBBY | 2D. FORTUNE | 3D. CATEGORY | 4D. SENTRIES
Mystery Answer: CHURCHGOERS

27. **Jumbles:** 2A. IDENTITY | 6A. EFFECTS | 7A. RALLY | 8A. RISES | 1D. DIRECTOR | 3D. EFFORTS | 4D. TACKLES | 5D. TASTY
Mystery Answer: FERTILE CRESCENT

28. **Jumbles:** 1A. KEEPERS | 5A. TOUGHEN | 6A. TWIGS | 7A. STRUGGLE | 1D. KITTENS | 2D. EQUATOR | 3D. ECHOING | 4D. SINUS
Mystery Answer: INHERITANCE

29. **Jumbles:** 1A. BUILDING | 4A. LEARNING | 6A. INTERVAL | 7A. MEETINGS | 1D. BELGIUM | 2D. LARGEST | 3D. GOGGLES | 5D. INVENT
Mystery Answer: GUARDIAN ANGEL

30. **Jumbles:** 1A. SYMBOL | 5A. OFTEN | 6A. SHAMPOO | 7A. SUSPENSE | 1D. SCHOLARS | 2D. MULTIPLE | 3D. OPINIONS | 4D. MISSES
Mystery Answer: MISSIONARY

31. **Jumbles:** 1A. ASPECT | 4A. CONFIRM | 5A. AFFORD | 6A. HELPLESS | 1D. ANNUALLY | 2D. PAINFUL | 3D. CAMERAS | 4D. COUGHS
Mystery Answer: DAMASCUS

32. **Jumbles:** 1A. WORRYING | 5A. INDICATE | 6A. NEEDING | 7A. SWINGING | 1D. WRITINGS | 2D. REDUCE | 3D. YACHTING | 4D. NITROGEN
Mystery Answer: CONSECRATE

33. **Jumbles:** 1A. REVIVAL | 5A. FUSES | 6A. BOTTLE | 7A. EXECUTED | 1D. REFERRED | 2D. VISIBLE | 3D. VISIT | 4D. LONELIER
Mystery Answer: BELIEVER

34. **Jumbles:** 1A. OUTLINE | 4A. JOURNEYS | 6A. CAPACITY | 7A. SATURDAY | 1D. OBJECTS | 2D. TRUMPET | 3D. EGYPTIAN | 5D. NICER
Mystery Answer: COMPASSION

35. **Jumbles:** 1A. COMPARES | 5A. OUTCOME | 6A. PROPERLY | 7A. DISCO | 1D. CHOPPED | 2D. METHODS | 3D. AROSE | 4D. EVENLY
Mystery Answer: SHEPHERD

36. **Jumbles:** 2A. STORM | 4A. INSIDE | 6A. HIMSELF | 7A. PANCAKES | 1D. KETCHUP | 2D. SHIPMENT | 3D. MODIFIED | 5D. SEESAW
Mystery Answer: OMNIPOTENT

37. **Jumbles:** 1A. HUMANOID | 6A. GADGETS | 7A. UNTYING | 8A. OUNCE | 2D. UNGLUED | 3D. ADDITION | 4D. OBEDIENT | 5D. DISAGREE
Mystery Answer: CONGREGATION

38. **Jumbles:** 2A. ESKIMOS | 6A. ACCUSES | 7A. DESPITE | 8A. DRAINED | 1D. REWARDED | 3D. KICKS | 4D. MISSION | 5D. SUSPEND
Mystery Answer: PEACEMAKERS

39. **Jumbles:** 1A. ROASTED | 5A. PLURAL | 6A. RAINFALL | 7A. UNCLES | 1D. REPORTER | 2D. ALUMINUM | 3D. TRAFFIC | 4D. SHELLS
Mystery Answer: SCRIPTURE

40. **Jumbles:** 1A. CLEARED | 5A. PLAGUE | 6A. REALIZE | 7A. NANNY | 1D. COVERING | 2D. EXPLAIN | 3D. READILY | 4D. DOUSE
Mystery Answer: EVANGELICAL

41. **Jumbles:** 1A. BUBBLING | 5A. ISLANDS | 6A. ANOTHER | 7A. NINES | 1D. BRITAIN | 2D. BALLOON | 3D. LUNCHES | 4D. NOSTRILS
Mystery Answer: THESSALONIANS

42. **Jumbles:** 1A. CHINESE | 5A. ADDED | 6A. INSPECTS | 7A. GERMS | 1D. COATING | 2D. INDUSTRY | 3D. ENDLESS | 4D. EQUATION
Mystery Answer: EASTER SUNDAY

43. **Jumbles:** 1A. ESCAPES | 5A. THIRST | 6A. NEGATIVE | 7A. SUPPORTS | 1D. EXTENDS | 2D. CLING | 3D. POSITION | 4D. SPEEDS
Mystery Answer: CHRISTIANS

44. **Jumbles:** 2A. COVERS | 5A. EXOTIC | 6A. FORWARD | 7A. SQUEEZES | 1D. GOLDFISH | 2D. CHEERFUL | 3D. VIOLATE | 4D. REINDEER
Mystery Answer: RIGHTEOUSNESS

45. **Jumbles:** 1A. CLASSIC | 5A. OUTLINES | 6A. DEVELOP | 7A. YOUNG | 1D. CROWDED | 2D. ACTIVITY | 3D. STILLS | 4D. CREEPING
Mystery Answer: PROTESTANTS

46. **Jumbles:** 1A. CHEAPEST | 5A. MAINS | 6A. EXPANDED | 7A. SUDDENLY | 1D. CLIMBERS | 2D. EQUIPPED | 3D. PRESENCE | 4D. THURSDAY
Mystery Answer: BLASPHEMY

47. **Jumbles:** 1A. ITALICS | 5A. FIERCELY | 6A. SHUDDER | 7A. EXTINCT | 1D. INFESTED | 2D. ADEQUATE | 3D. INCIDENT | 4D. SOLAR
Mystery Answer: SANCTIFICATION

48. **Jumbles:** 2A. DRESS | 5A. STUMBLED | 7A. RELAXED | 8A. EXCUSING | 1D. OBSERVER | 3D. SPENDING | 4D. PUBLIC | 6D. BOXES
Mystery Answer: CONVERSION

49. **Jumbles:** 1A. YACHT | 6A. UMBRELLA | 7A. MUSTACHE | 8A. TOURISTS | 2D. COLLECTS | 3D. THEATERS | 4D. SUMMIT | 5D. WRITER
Mystery Answer: ECCLESIASTES

50. **Jumbles:** 2A. LESSER | 5A. FAITHFUL | 7A. JUNGLE | 8A. WEAKNESS | 1D. CLIFFS | 3D. REFUGEE | 4D. VALUE | 6D. TRUNK
Mystery Answer: TREASURE

51. **Jumbles:** 1. JERICHO | 2. MARCHING | 3. GOSHEN |
4. GIBEONITES | 5. CONQUEST
Mystery Answer: JOSHUA

52. **Jumbles:** 1. VASHTI | 2. MORDECAI | 3. HAMAN |
4. BANQUETS | 5. QUEEN
Mystery Answer: ESTHER

53. **Jumbles:** 1. HEBREWS | 2. NILE RIVER | 3. LOCUSTS |
4. PLAGUES | 5. HARDENED
Mystery Answer: PHARAOH

54. **Jumbles:** 1. WISDOM | 2. SPLENDOR | 3. TEMPLE |
4. SHEBA | 5. ROYALTY
Mystery Answer: SOLOMON

55. **Jumbles:** 1. BETRAYAL | 2. BARABBAS | 3. PARDON |
4. CRUCIFY | 5. GOLGOTHA
Mystery Answer: PILATE

56. **Jumbles:** 1. ZECHARIAH | 2. BAPTIZED | 3. GABRIEL |
4. BARREN | 5. PREGNANT
Mystery Answer: ELIZABETH

57. **Jumbles:** 1. PROPHETESS | 2. MOSES | 3. DISEASE |
4. TAMBOURINE | 5. DANCING
Mystery Answer: MIRIAM

58. **Jumbles:** 1. DREAMS | 2. PROPHET | 3. EPIPHANY |
4. ADONIJAH | 5. SOLOMON
Mystery Answer: NATHAN

59. **Jumbles:** 1. GALILEE | 2. FOLLOWER | 3. SPICES | 4. BURIAL |
5. ALARM
Mystery Answer: SALOME

60. **Jumbles:** 1. EPHRAIM | 2. CANAANITE | 3. PLUNDER |
4. BARAK | 5. MORALITY
Mystery Answer: DEBORAH

61. **Jumbles:** 1. LAZARUS | 2. HOSTESS | 3. RESURRECT |
4. COMFORT | 5. BETHANY
Mystery Answer: MARTHA

62. **Jumbles:** 1. BEAUTIFUL | 2. ADULTERESS | 3. ROOFTOP |
4. URIAH | 5. HUSBAND
Mystery Answer: BATHSHEBA

63. **Jumbles:** 1. CUPBEARER | 2. POTIPHAR | 3. BROTHERS |
4. JACKET | 5. ISHMAELITES
Mystery Answer: JOSEPH

64. **Jumbles:** 1. BILHAH | 2. DECEPTION | 3. FOURTEEN |
4. PASTURE | 5. JOSEPH
Mystery Answer: RACHEL

65. **Jumbles:** 1. FURNACE | 2. HANANIAH | 3. UNDEFILED |
4. COURTS | 5. BABYLON
Mystery Answer: SHADRACH

66. **Jumbles:** 1. FRIENDSHIP | 2. LOYALTY | 3. JOURNEY |
4. FESTIVAL | 5. ARCHERY
Mystery Answer: JONATHAN

67. **Jumbles:** 1. SALVATION | 2. RIGHTEOUS | 3. JUSTICE |
4. COUNSEL | 5. PEACE
Mystery Answer: JESUS

68. **Jumbles:** 1. DISCIPLE | 2. ZEALOT | 3. MARTYRED |
4. FISHERMAN | 5. ROOSTERS
Mystery Answer: PETER

69. **Jumbles:** 1. MUSCLES | 2. RIDDLES | 3. PHILISTINES |
4. AMBUSH | 5. RAZOR
Mystery Answer: SAMSON

70. **Jumbles:** 1. DEACONS | 2. APOSTLE | 3. DETAINED |
4. STONING | 5. SANHEDRIN
Mystery Answer: STEPHEN

71. **Jumbles:** 1. MISSING | 2. WORSHIP | 3. DOUBTER |
4. TWELVE | 5. MIRACULOUS
Mystery Answer: THOMAS

72. **Jumbles:** 1. LIFETIME | 2. OUTLIVE | 3. HUNDREDS |
4. LAMECH | 5. CHILDREN
Mystery Answer: METHUSELAH

73. **Jumbles:** 1. MOUNTAIN | 2. FATHER | 3. GOMORRAH |
4. ABIMELECH | 5. ISHMAEL
Mystery Answer: ABRAHAM

74. **Jumbles:** 1. MIRACLE | 2. MOURNED | 3. ANOINTING |
4. DEMONS | 5. SUNDAY
Mystery Answer: MARY MAGDALENE

75. **Jumbles:** 1. EPHESIANS | 2. INSTRUCTIONS |
3. MISSIONARY | 4. OFFERING | 5. LYSTRA
Mystery Answer: TIMOTHY

PSALM JUMBLES

76. **Jumbles:** 1. CHAFF | 2. TREES | 3. WICKED | 4. WITHER |
5. PLANTED | 6. MOCKERS
Mystery Answer: LORD WATCHES

77. **Jumbles:** 1. VALLEY | 2. CLOSE | 3. GOODNESS |
4. SHEPHERD | 5. UNFAILING | 6. OVERFLOWS
Mystery Answer: PEACEFUL

78. **Jumbles:** 1. SHOUT | 2. PROMISED | 3. ENEMIES |
4. PUTTING | 5. EVERYONE | 6. ASCENDED
Mystery Answer: POSSESSION

79. **Jumbles:** 1. BOAST | 2. MIGHTY | 3. RAZOR | 4. LAUGH |
5. TONGUE | 6. DESTRUCTION
Mystery Answer: AMAZED

80. **Jumbles:** 1. HELPER | 2. TRYING | 3. TRIUMPH |
4. PROMISED | 5. STRANGERS | 6. ATTACKING
Mystery Answer: PRAYER

81. **Jumbles:** 1. PRAYER | 2. TOWERING | 3. FORTRESS |
4. GENERATIONS | 5. OVERWHELMED | 6. FAITHFULNESS
Mystery Answer: SHELTER [OF YOUR] WINGS

82. **Jumbles:** 1. SHAME | 2. NEEDY | 3. PLEASE | 4. TROUBLE |
5. HUMILIATED | 6. REPEATEDLY
Mystery Answer: HELPER

83. **Jumbles:** 1. ABOUT | 2. HEAVENLY | 3. IGNORANT |
4. OPPRESSED | 5. DESTITUTE | 6. PRONOUNCES
Mystery Answer: NATIONS BELONG

84. **Jumbles:** 1. SHADOW | 2. REFUGE | 3. SAFETY | 4. SHELTER |
5. ALMIGHTY | 6. PROTECTION
Mystery Answer: FEATHERS

85. **Jumbles:** 1. POWER | 2. JOYFUL | 3. VICTORY |
4. WONDERFUL | 5. REMEMBERED | 6. RIGHTEOUSNESS
Mystery Answer: SYMPHONY

86. **Jumbles:** 1. PASTURE | 2. WORSHIP | 3. GLADNESS |
4. GENERATION | 5. ACKNOWLEDGE | 6. THANKSGIVING
Mystery Answer: LOVE CONTINUES

87. **Jumbles:** 1. HONOR | 2. FOOTSTOOL | 3. EXTEND |
4. ARRAYED | 5. WILLINGLY | 6. MELCHIZEDEK
Mystery Answer: RIGHT HAND

88. **Jumbles:** 1. ENTIRE | 2. WEALTHY | 3. COMMANDS |
4. SUCCESSFUL | 5. GENEROUS | 6. BUSINESS
Mystery Answer: FEARLESS

89. **Jumbles:** 1. AGAIN | 2. ACCEPT | 3. BALANCE | 4. PROMISE |
5. RIGHTEOUS | 6. DETERMINED
Mystery Answer: INSTRUCTIONS

90. **Jumbles:** 1. BESIDE | 2. HEAVEN | 3. HIMSELF |
4. MOUNTAINS | 5. SLUMBERS | 6. PROTECTIVE
Mystery Answer: FOREVER

91. **Jumbles:** 1. QUIVER | 2. ACCUSERS | 3. PROTECTS |
4. BUILDERS | 5. GUARDING | 6. ANXIOUSLY
Mystery Answer: SENTRIES

92. **Jumbles:** 1. PEACE | 2. LABOR | 3. PROSPER |
4. CHILDREN | 5. FRUITFUL | 6. FLOURISHING
Mystery Answer: AROUND [YOUR] TABLE

93. **Jumbles:** 1. REFUSE | 2. YOUTH | 3. ENEMIES | 4. PLOWED |
5. UNGODLY | 6. COVERED
Mystery Answer: PERSECUTED

94. **Jumbles:** 1. REDEEM | 2. HIMSELF | 3. SURVIVE |
4. COUNTING | 5. ATTENTION | 6. OVERFLOWS
Mystery Answer: FORGIVENESS

95. **Jumbles:** 1. PRAYER | 2. HERMON | 3. PLEASANT |
4. BROTHERS | 5. REFRESHING | 6. PRONOUNCED
Mystery Answer: HARMONY

96. **Jumbles:** 1. OCEANS | 2. SPIRIT | 3. SUPPORT |
4. EXAMINED | 5. FARTHEST | 6. DARKNESS
Mystery Answer: PRESENCE

97. **Jumbles:** 1. INNER | 2. COMPLEX | 3. DELICATE |
4. OUTNUMBER | 5. SECLUSION | 6. SINGLE
Mystery Answer: PRECIOUS

98. **Jumbles:** 1. GUARD | 2. HURRY | 3. CONTROL |
4. DELICACIES | 5. CONSTANTLY | 6. UPRAISED
Mystery Answer: SOOTHING

99. **Jumbles:** 1. BEYOND | 2. THANKS | 3. ABSOLUTE |
4. REBUILDING | 5. DELIGHTFUL | 6. PRAISES
Mystery Answer: BROKENHEARTED

100. **Jumbles:** 1. BREATHES | 2. GREATNESS | 3. CYMBALS |
4. TAMBOURINE | 5. DANCING | 6. EVERYTHING
Mystery Answer: SANCTUARY

WHO SAID THAT? JUMBLES

101. **Jumbles:** 1. HIGH PRIEST *(Mark 14:60)* | 2. ZECHARIAH
(Luke 1:18) | 3. ELIZABETH *(Luke 1:25)* | 4. ANGELS *(Luke
2:14)* | 5. NATHANAEL *(John 1:49)* | 6. NICODEMUS *(John 7:51)*

102. **Jumbles:** 1. PHARISEES *(Matthew 9:11)* | 2. JOHN[']S
DISCIPLES *(Luke 7:19)* | 3. PILATE[']S WIFE *(Matthew 27:19)* |
4. HERODIAS *(Mark 6:24)* | 5. SADDUCEES *(Luke 20:28)* |
6. APOSTLE PAUL *(Philippians 4:4-5, NIV)*

103. **Jumbles:** 1. RAHAB *(Joshua 2:5)* | 2. PHINEHAS *(Joshua
22:31)* | 3. ACSAH *(Judges 1:15)* | 4. DEBORAH *(Judges 4:9)* |
5. GIDEON *(Judges 7:15)* | 6. JOTHAM *(Judges 9:7-8)*

104. **Jumbles:** 1. MOSES *(Deuteronomy 6:4-5, NIV)* | 2. JOSHUA
(Joshua 24:23) | 3. KING DAVID *(2 Samuel 7:18)* |
4. ZACCHAEUS *(Luke 19:8)* | 5. SIMON PETER *(Mark 14:71)* |
6. PHILIP *(John 6:7, NIV)*

105. **Jumbles:** 1. ROMANS *(Romans 1:20)* | 2. DEUTERONOMY
(Deuteronomy 7:7) | 3. PROVERBS *(Proverbs 27:19)* |

4. REVELATION *(Revelation 21:5)* | 5. PSALMS *(Psalm 141:3)* |
6. JAMES (JAMES 4:7)

106. **Jumbles:** 1. HAGGAI *(Haggai 2:15)* | 2. SECOND KINGS
(2 Kings 12:16) | 3. EXODUS *(Exodus 27:1-2)* | 4. HEBREWS
(Hebrews 10:23) | 5. MATTHEW *(Matthew 5:6)* | 6. NUMBERS
(Numbers 10:35)

107. **Jumbles:** 1. GALATIANS *(Galatians 5:22-23)* | 2. SECOND
TIMOTHY *(2 Timothy 3:16)* | 3. SONG OF SONGS *(Song of
Songs 2:1)* | 4. FIRST SAMUEL *(1 Samuel 26:23)* | 5. GENESIS
(Genesis 6:11) | 6. FIRST CORINTHIANS *(1 Corinthians 3:6)*

108. **Jumbles:** 1. LEGION *(Mark 5:7)* | 2. MARTHA *(Luke 10:40)* |
3. CLEOPAS *(Luke 24:18)* | 4. SAMARITAN WOMAN *(John
4:15)* | 5. CAIAPHAS *(John 11:49-50)* | 6. JOHN THE BAPTIST
(John 1:27)

109. **Jumbles:** 1. SOLOMON *(1 Kings 3:9)* | 2. ELISHA *(2 Kings 2:9)* |
3. KING JOASH *(2 Kings 12:7)* | 4. GEDALIAH *(2 Kings 25:24)* |

5. JEHOSHAPHAT *(2 Chronicles 20:6)* | 6. NEHEMIAH *(Nehemiah 2:17)*

110. **Jumbles:** 1. OBADIAH *(Obadiah 1:12)* | 2. HOSEA *(Hosea 6:1)* | 3. MICAH *(Micah 7:14)* | 4. JONAH *(Jonah 4:2)* | 5. HABAKKUK *(Habakkuk 2:14)* | 6. MALACHI *(Malachi 2:15)*

111. **Jumbles:** 1. JAMES *(James 1:19)* | 2. TERTULLUS *(Acts 24:2)* | 3. CORNELIUS *(Acts 10:33)* | 4. STEPHEN *(Acts 7:56)* | 5. GAMALIEL *(Acts 5:35)* | 6. SIMON THE SORCERER *(Acts 8:19)*

112. **Jumbles:** 1. ANANIAS *(Acts 9:17)* | 2. LYDIA *(Acts 16:15)* | 3. GALLIO *(Acts 18:14)* | 4. FESTUS *(Acts 25:9)* | 5. AGRIPPA *(Acts 26:32)* | 6. JAMES AND JOHN *(Mark 10:37)*

113. **Jumbles:** 1. ABIMELECH *(Judges 9:54, NIV)* | 2. JEPHTHAH *(Judges 11:30-31)* | 3. MANOAH *(Judges 13:8)* | 4. DELILAH *(Judges 16:10)* | 5. NAOMI *(Ruth 1:9)* | 6. HANNAH *(1 Samuel 2:1)*

114. **Jumbles:** 1. SAMUEL *(1 Samuel 3:10)* | 2. NATHAN *(2 Samuel 12:13-14)* | 3. JONADAB *(2 Samuel 13:4)* | 4. AMNON *(2 Samuel 13:4)* | 5. ABSALOM *(2 Samuel 14:32)* | 6. AHITHOPHEL *(2 Samuel 17:1-2)*

115. **Jumbles:** 1. HADAD *(1 Kings 11:21)* | 2. AHIJAH *(1 Kings 11:31)* | 3. REHOBOAM *(2 Chronicles 10:9)* | 4. JEROBOAM *(1 Kings 14:2)* | 5. ELIJAH *(1 KINGS 18:21)* | 6. JEZEBEL *(1 Kings 21:7)*

116. **Jumbles:** 1. MORDECAI *(Esther 4:14)* | 2. QUEEN ESTHER *(Esther 7:3)* | 3. KING XERXES *(Esther 5:3)* | 4. HAMAN *(Esther 6:6)* | 5. ETHAN *(Psalm 89:1)* | 6. ABRAHAM *(Genesis 22:8)*

117. **Jumbles:** 1. JUDGES *(Judges 5:31)* | 2. PHILIPPIANS *(Philippians 2:5)* | 3. ECCLESIASTES *(Ecclesiastes 12:13)* | 4. EPHESIANS *(Ephesians 2:13)* | 5. TITUS *(Titus 3:1)* | 6. LAMENTATIONS *(Lamentations 3:22)*

118. **Jumbles:** 1. ABIGAIL *(1 Samuel 25:24-25)* | 2. JACOB *(Genesis 48:3)* | 3. JEREMIAH *(Jeremiah 1:6)* | 4. PONTIUS PILATE *(Luke 23:14)* | 5. ANGEL OF THE LORD *(Luke 2:10-11)* | 6. SIMEON *(Luke 2:29-30)*

119. **Jumbles:** 1. JAIRUS *(Mark 5:23)* | 2. BARTIMAEUS *(Mark 10:47, 51)* | 3. JUDAS ISCARIOT *(Matthew 26:48)* | 4. SOLDIERS *(Matthew 27:29)* | 5. SARAI *(Genesis 16:5)* | 6. RACHEL *(Genesis 30:8)*

120. **Jumbles:** 1. SHECHEM *(Genesis 34:11-12)* | 2. JOSEPH *(Genesis 37:16)* | 3. CUPBEARER *(Genesis 40:9-10)* | 4. PHARAOH *(Exodus 5:17)* | 5. SAMSON *(Judges 15:16)* | 6. JONATHAN *(1 Samuel 14:29)*

121. **Jumbles:** 1. ELIPHAZ *(Job 4:6)* | 2. ASAPH *(Psalm 79:9)* | 3. ISAIAH *(Isaiah 40:3)* | 4. EZEKIEL *(Ezekiel 12:3)* | 5. NEBUCHADNEZZAR *(Daniel 4:3)* | 6. DANIEL *(Daniel 6:22)*

122. **Jumbles:** 1. ZEPHANIAH *(Zephaniah 1:7)* | 2. ZECHARIAH *(Zechariah 1:18-19)* | 3. MALACHI *(Malachi 2:10)* | 4. KING HEROD *(Matthew 2:8)* | 5. THE DEVIL *(Matthew 4:3)* | 6. CENTURION *(Matthew 8:8)*

123. **Jumbles:** 1. BARZILLAI *(2 Samuel 19:34)* | 2. MEPHIBOSHETH *(2 Samuel 19:30)* | 3. BATHSHEBA *(1 Kings 1:31)* | 4. BENAIAH *(1 Kings 1:36-37)* | 5. HIRAM *(1 Kings 5:7)* | 6. QUEEN OF SHEBA *(1 Kings 10:6-7)*

124. **Jumbles:** 1. MICAIAH *(1 Kings 22:17)* | 2. NAAMAN *(2 Kings 5:11)* | 3. HAZAEL *(2 Kings 8:13)* | 4. JEHOIADA *(2 Kings 11:15)* | 5. ELIAKIM *(2 Kings 18:26)* | 6. HEZEKIAH *(2 Kings 19:16)*

125. **Jumbles:** 1. COLOSSIANS *(Colossians 2:5)* | 2. SECOND CHRONICLES *(2 Chronicles 28:14)* | 3. LEVITICUS *(Leviticus 16:34)* | 4. THIRD JOHN *(3 John 1:11)* | 5. SECOND SAMUEL *(2 Samuel 19:14)* | 6. PHILEMON *(Philemon 1:4)*

BOX OF CLUES JUMBLES

126. **Jumbles:** 1. EVE | 2. ADAM | 3. GRASS | 4. CATTLE | 5. FORBADE | 6. BREATHES | 7. FIRMAMENT | 8. MULTIPLIED
Mystery Answer: FIRST GARDEN

127. **Jumbles:** 1. JEW | 2. VINE | 3. CHIEF | 4. SAVIOR | 5. JEHOVAH | 6. ADVOCATE | 7. COUNSELOR | 8. REDEMPTION
Mystery Answer: CORNERSTONE

128. **Jumbles:** 1. RED | 2. TRUE | 3. LIGHT | 4. WISDOM | 5. OBADIAH | 6. LEVITICUS | 7. NEHEMIAH | 8. CHRONICLES
Mystery Answer: OLD TESTAMENT

129. **Jumbles:** 1. SON | 2. POOR | 3. PROUD | 4. PRINCE | 5. PERFECT | 6. VIRTUOUS | 7. HYPOCRITE | 8. TALEBEARER
Mystery Answer: PEOPLE [OF] PROVERBS

130. **Jumbles:** 1. CUP | 2. HEAD | 3. HOUSE | 4. PURSUE | 5. ENEMIES | 6. MEADOWS | 7. GOODNESS | 8. OVERFLOWS
Mystery Answer: SHEPHERD[']S PSALM

131. **Jumbles:** 1. INN | 2. ANNA | 3. PEACE | 4. TIDINGS | 5. GABRIEL | 6. SHEPHERD | 7. BETHLEHEM | 8. SWADDLING
Mystery Answer: CHRISTMAS

132. **Jumbles:** 1. OLD | 2. SINAI | 3. AARON | 4. JOSHUA | 5. PLAGUES | 6. SACRIFICE | 7. CUCUMBER | 8. WILDERNESS
Mystery Answer: WANDERINGS

133. **Jumbles:** 1. ARK | 2. BULLS | 3. PEOPLE | 4. REDEEM | 5. RAINBOW | 6. ESTABLISH | 7. COVENANT | 8. GENERATION
Mystery Answer: GOD[']S PROMISES

134. **Jumbles:** 1. RAM | 2. GIFT | 3. PEACE | 4. PIGEON | 5. HEIFER | 6. INCENSE | 7. PERSONAL | 8. TURTLEDOVE
Mystery Answer: SACRIFICES

135. **Jumbles:** 1. CRY | 2. FOUND | 3. MOCKED | 4. WHIPPED | 5. VINEGAR | 6. GOLGOTHA | 7. SIXTH HOUR | 8. GETHSEMANE
Mystery Answer: CRUCIFIXION

136. **Jumbles:** 1. SEE | 2. PRAY | 3. CLOAK | 4. DONKEY | 5. HOSANNA | 6. BRANCHES | 7. JERUSALEM | 8. INSTRUCTED
Mystery Answer: TRIUMPHAL ENTRY

137. **Jumbles:** 1. JOY | 2. JOHN | 3. SEVEN | 4. PATMOS | 5. WITNESS | 6. FINE LINEN | 7. DOXOLOGY | 8. WHITE HORSE
Mystery Answer: REVELATION

138. **Jumbles:** 1. MEN | 2. COME | 3. VISION | 4. FRIGHTEN | 5. MORNING | 6. THIRD DAY | 7. MAGDALENE | 8. EARTHQUAKE
Mystery Answer: RESURRECTION

139. **Jumbles:** 1. LOVE | 2. FAITH | 3. PURITY | 4. HUMILITY | 5. OBEDIENCE | 6. REVERENCE | 7. GENTLENESS | 8. SELF-CONTROL
Mystery Answer: GODLY TRAITS

140. **Jumbles:** 1. CON | 2. KILL | 3. POACH | 4. MURDER | 5. IDOLIZE | 6. ADULTERY | 7. PROFANITY | 8. COVETOUSNESS
Mystery Answer: YOU SHALL NOT

141. **Jumbles:** 1. WAY | 2. WISE | 3. GLORY | 4. VIRTUE | 5. BLESSED | 6. JUDGMENT | 7. KNOWLEDGE | 8. MESSENGERS
Mystery Answer: WORDS [OF] WISDOM

142. **Jumbles:** 1. JOB | 2. PAUL | 3. MOSES | 4. CHRIST | 5. ABRAHAM | 6. JONATHAN | 7. ZECHARIAH | 8. METHUSELAH
Mystery Answer: BIBLE HEROES

143. **Jumbles:** 1. RED | 2. CITY | 3. HAZOR | 4. GILEAD | 5. MEGIDDO | 6. NAZARETH | 7. DAMASCUS | 8. CAPPADOCIA
Mystery Answer: GEOGRAPHY

144. **Jumbles:** 1. ESAU | 2. STONE | 3. BETHEL | 4. PROMISE | 5. JOURNEY | 6. PROVIDED | 7. STAIRWAY | 8. DESCENDANT
Mystery Answer: JACOB['] S LADDER

145. **Jumbles:** 1. SIN | 2. FIBS | 3. COVET | 4. MURDER | 5. GLUTTONY | 6. JEALOUSIES | 7. BLASPHEMY | 8. DEBAUCHERY
Mystery Answer: ABOMINATIONS

146. **Jumbles:** 1. OUR | 2. GLORY | 3. BREAD | 4. HEAVEN | 5. DEBTORS | 6. FORGIVEN | 7. HALLOWED | 8. TEMPTATION
Mystery Answer: LORD['] S PRAYER

147. **Jumbles:** 1. ASA | 2. JEHU | 3. ABDON | 4. GIDEON | 5. SHAMGAR | 6. HEZEKIAH | 7. JEHOIAKIM | 8. BELSHAZZAR
Mystery Answer: KINGS [AND] JUDGES

148. **Jumbles:** 1. AGE | 2. HELP | 3. IMAGE | 4. ANSWER | 5. FURNACE | 6. INNOCENT | 7. OVERPOWER | 8. KING DARIUS
Mystery Answer: LIONS['] DEN

149. **Jumbles:** 1. YOU | 2. ITCH | 3. GUILT | 4. ATONES | 5. EVENING | 6. CLEANSING | 7. UNLAWFUL | 8. PUNISHMENT
Mystery Answer: LEVITICUS

150. **Jumbles:** 1. KEY | 2. HAND | 3. ASAPH | 4. TOBIAH | 5. TRUMPET | 6. BREACHES | 7. CAPTIVITY | 8. REMEMBERED
Mystery Answer: NEHEMIAH

TRIVIA JUMBLES

151. **Jumbles:** 1. JAMES | 2. MATTHEW | 3. HEBREWS | 4. TIMOTHY | 5. CORINTHIANS
Mystery Answer: NEW TESTAMENT

152. **Jumbles:** 1. PETER | 2. PHILIP | 3. SIMON | 4. THOMAS | 5. ANDREW
Mystery Answer: APOSTLES

153. **Jumbles:** 1. EGYPTIANS | 2. PHARISEES | 3. SADDUCEES | 4. MESOPOTAMIANS | 5. BABYLONIANS
Mystery Answer: PEOPLE GROUPS

154. **Jumbles:** 1. HUMBLE | 2. UPRIGHT | 3. LOVING | 4. SINCERE | 5. FAITHFUL
Mystery Answer: [THE] CHRISTIAN [LIFE]

155. **Jumbles:** 1. GLORY | 2. MERCIFUL | 3. JUDGMENT | 4. EVERYWHERE | 5. COMPASSIONATE
Mystery Answer: GOD['] S CHARACTER

156. **Jumbles:** 1. HIVITES | 2. ASSYRIANS | 3. AMORITES | 4. AMALEKITES | 5. HITTITES
Mystery Answer: ENEMIES

157. **Jumbles:** 1. CLERGY | 2. PASTOR | 3. BISHOP | 4. MESSENGER | 5. EVANGELISTS
Mystery Answer: MINISTRY

158. **Jumbles:** 1. SHEEP | 2. TALENTS | 3. PRODIGAL | 4. LABORERS | 5. RICH FOOL
Mystery Answer: CHRIST['] S PARABLES

159. **Jumbles:** 1. THUNDER | 2. OVERCOMES | 3. RAINBOW | 4. LIGHTNING | 5. EMERALD
Mystery Answer: [THE] THRONE [IN] HEAVEN

160. **Jumbles:** 1. WRATH | 2. SCORNS | 3. REBELLION | 4. UNKINDNESS | 5. TRANSGRESSIONS
Mystery Answer: WICKEDNESS

161. **Jumbles:** 1. BABEL | 2. DIVINE | 3. BOANERGES | 4. CHRISTIAN | 5. FIRMAMENT
Mystery Answer: BIBLE DEFINITIONS

162. **Jumbles:** 1. FALCON | 2. VULTURE | 3. BITTERNS | 4. SPARROW | 5. HUMMINGBIRD
Mystery Answer: [THEY ARE] FOWL [OF THE] BIBLE

163. **Jumbles:** 1. LIGHTS | 2. BELOVED | 3. BELIEVERS | 4. FRIENDS | 5. CHOSEN ONES
Mystery Answer: CHILDREN OF GOD

164. **Jumbles:** 1. FATHER | 2. SAVIOR | 3. WONDERFUL | 4. GREAT PHYSICIAN | 5. PRINCE OF PEACE
Mystery Answer: HOLY SPIRIT

165. **Jumbles:** 1. ENEMY | 2. TEMPTER | 3. ACCUSER | 4. APOLLYON | 5. FATHER OF LIES
Mystery Answer: NAMES OF SATAN

166. **Jumbles:** 1. HAPPY | 2. BLESSED | 3. INHERIT | 4. HUNGER | 5. COMFORTED
Mystery Answer: [THE] BEATITUDES

167. **Jumbles:** 1. TRUTH | 2. PATIENT | 3. REJOICES | 4. NEVER FAILS | 5. DOES NOT ENVY
Mystery Answer: [LOVE] PERSEVERES

168. **Jumbles:** 1. SEASON | 2. COUNSEL | 3. PROSPERS | 4. MEDITATE | 5. DELIGHTING
Mystery Answer: RIGHTEOUS

169. **Jumbles:** 1. HERDSMAN | 2. MISSIONARY | 3. CARPENTER | 4. CUPBEARER | 5. TAX COLLECTOR
Mystery Answer: OCCUPATIONS

170. **Jumbles:** 1. COVENANT | 2. IDOLATRY | 3. ATONEMENT | 4. REBELLIOUS | 5. HOLY LAND
Mystery Answer: DEUTERONOMY

171. **Jumbles:** 1. PLAGUES | 2. FIRSTBORN | 3. PHARAOH | 4. LIVESTOCK | 5. DARKNESS
Mystery Answer: ANGEL OF DEATH

172. **Jumbles:** 1. TEMPLE | 2. BAPTISM | 3. PREACHING | 4. CRUCIFIED | 5. RESURRECTION
Mystery Answer: CHRIST[']S LIFE

173. **Jumbles:** 1. RESTORE | 2. REDEEMED | 3. AFFECTION | 4. COMPASSIONS | 5. FAITHFULNESS
Mystery Answer: LAMENTATIONS

174. **Jumbles:** 1. FRUIT | 2. SERPENTS | 3. DOMINION | 4. KNOWLEDGE | 5. ADAM AND EVE
Mystery Answer: GARDEN OF EDEN

175. **Jumbles:** 1. TYRE AND SIDON | 2. BETHANY | 3. NAZARETH | 4. DAMASCUS | 5. SEA OF GALILEE
Mystery Answer: HOLY LAND

FIND THE JUMBLE

176. **Jumbles:** 1. CREATURES | 2. DOMINION | 3. FRUITFUL | 4. SEASONS | 5. WOMAN | 6. BEGINNING

178. **Jumbles:** 1. GLEANED | 2. HARVEST | 3. REAPERS | 4. HANDMAID | 5. WINNOW | 6. KINSMAN

177. **Jumbles:** 1. COMMAND | 2. COUNSEL | 3. REDEEM | 4. RESTORE | 5. INTERCEDE | 6. SUSTAIN

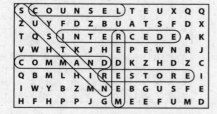

179. **Jumbles:** 1. JONAH | 2. NINEVEH | 3. TARSHISH | 4. DISTRESS | 5. JOPPA | 6. PRAYER

180. Jumbles: 1. SOLOMON | 2. WISDOM | 3. TEMPLE | 4. PALACE | 5. KINGDOM | 6. DAVID

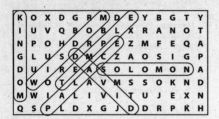

184. Jumbles: 1. SHEKEL | 2. CUBIT | 3. HOMER | 4. DENARIUS | 5. EPHAH | 6. HANDBREADTH

181. Jumbles: 1. QUAIL | 2. MANNA | 3. GRUMBLING | 4. WATER | 5. STAFF | 6. SPRINGS

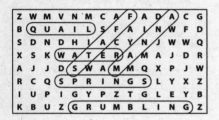

185. Jumbles: 1. HEBRON | 2. TARSUS | 3. SAMARIA | 4. ANTIOCH | 5. BETHANY | 6. GOMORRAH

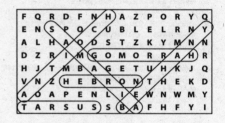

182. Jumbles: 1. PARABLE | 2. ORACLE | 3. PROPHECY | 4. GOSPEL | 5. EPISTLE | 6. ALLEGORY

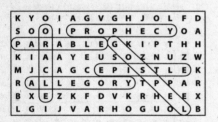

186. Jumbles: 1. BARNABAS | 2. LAZARUS | 3. ELIJAH | 4. JETHRO | 5. JEROBOAM | 6. PHILEMON

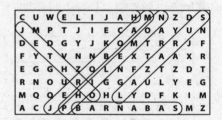

183. Jumbles: 1. GOSSIP | 2. JEALOUSY | 3. WITCHCRAFT | 4. GLUTTONY | 5. LYING | 6. MURDER

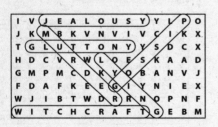

187. Jumbles: 1. JUDAS | 2. BETRAYAL | 3. TORTURE | 4. MOCKERY | 5. PARADISE | 6. THIEF

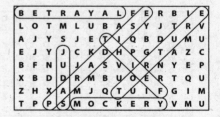

208

188. Jumbles: 1. SQUALL | 2. WAVES | 3. FAITH | 4. DISCIPLES | 5. REBUKE | 6. AFRAID

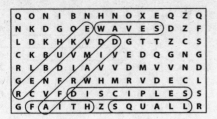

192. Jumbles: 1. PSALMS | 2. EZEKIEL | 3. PROVERBS | 4. JOSHUA | 5. CHRONICLES | 6. ISAIAH

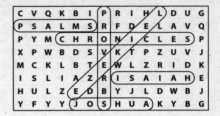

189. Jumbles: 1. CROWD | 2. GRASS | 3. LOAVES | 4. BASKETS | 5. SATISFIED | 6. MULTIPLIED

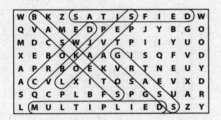

193. Jumbles: 1. PATMOS | 2. TIMOTHY | 3. JOURNEY | 4. PRISON | 5. HEBREWS | 6. COURAGE

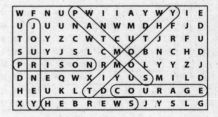

190. Jumbles: 1. IMMANUEL | 2. JEHOVAH | 3. MESSIAH | 4. KING OF KINGS | 5. COUNSELOR | 6. ALMIGHTY

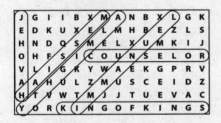

194. Jumbles: 1. GOLIATH | 2. DELILAH | 3. BARABBAS | 4. ANANIAS | 5. KING SAUL | 6. PHARAOH

191. Jumbles: 1. MARTHA | 2. HANNAH | 3. ELIZABETH | 4. EUNICE | 5. HAGAR | 6. SALOME

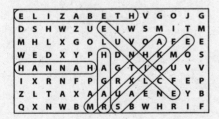

195. Jumbles: 1. PEACE | 2. PATIENCE | 3. GENTLENESS | 4. GOODNESS | 5. SELF-CONTROL | 6. KINDNESS

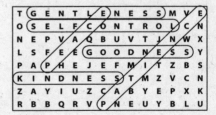

196. Jumbles: 1. SAVING | 2. OMNISCIENT | 3. GLORIFIED | 4. JUDGE | 5. GRACIOUS | 6. FORGIVING

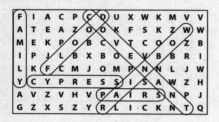

199. Jumbles: 1. CAMELS | 2. BULLOCKS | 3. CHEESES | 4. CHARIOTS | 5. PILLARS | 6. CURTAINS

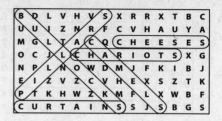

197. Jumbles: 1. COVENANT | 2. FLOOD | 3. PAIRS | 4. RAINBOW | 5. FAMILY | 6. CYPRESS

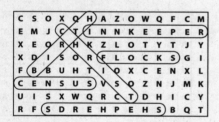

200. Jumbles: 1. TALENTS | 2. POUNDS | 3. WIDOW | 4. LABORERS | 5. TREASURE | 6. FIG TREE

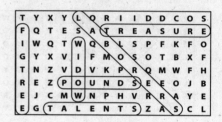

198. Jumbles: 1. BIRTH | 2. CENSUS | 3. SHEPHERDS | 4. INNKEEPER | 5. FLOCKS | 6. CHRIST

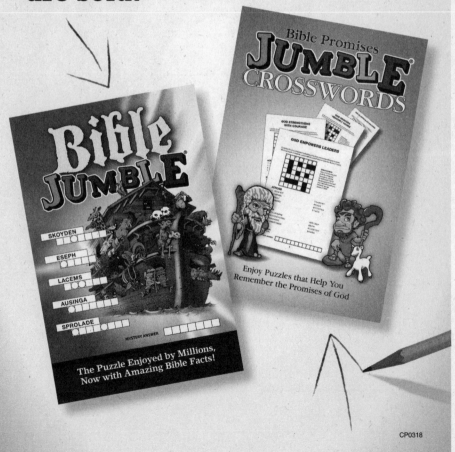